A Tale of Two Fiddlers

The Early Days of Sports and Life in Charlottetown

FRED MACDONALD

ACORNPRESS

ACORNPRESS

Acorn Press
PO Box 22024
Charlottetown, PE
C1A 9J2
Acornpresscanada.com

Printed in Canada
Design by Cassandra Aragonez
Edited by Lee Ellen Pottie
Copy edit by Jennifer Graham

Library and Archives Canada Cataloguing in Publication
Title: A tale of two Fiddlers: the early days of sports and life in Charlottetown / by Fred MacDonald.
Names: MacDonald, Fred (Sportswriter), author.
Identifiers: Canadiana (print) 20200224050 |
Canadiana (ebook) 20200224204 |
ISBN 9781773660486 (softcover) | ISBN 9781773660530 (HTML)

Subjects: LCSH: MacDonald, Fred (Sportswriter) | LCSH: MacDonald, James L. Fiddler. | LCSH: MacDonald, Fred (Sportswriter)—Family. | LCSH: MacDonald, Fred (Sportswriter)—Childhood and youth. | LCSH: Charlottetown (P.E.I.)—Social life and customs—20th century. | LCSH: Sports— Prince Edward Island—Charlottetown— History—20th century. | LCSH: Sportswriters—Prince Edward Island—Charlottetown—Biography. | LCGFT: Autobiographies. Classification: LCC FC2646.26.M33 A3 2020 | DDC 971.7/504092—dc23

The publisher acknowledges the support of the Government of Canada, The Canada Council for the Arts and the Province of Prince Edward Island.

In loving memory of my mother and father,
Pat and Fiddler, and a gift to my brothers and sisters.

Contents

CHAPTER 1

First Recollections

MY FIRST RECOLLECTION OF CHARLOTTETOWN IN
the mid-1950s was living on Fitzroy Street just up from the old
Charlottetown Forum across the street from MacIntyre's store
on the corner now occupied by the Perfection Foods building.
I was about eight or nine, but I remember a little pond in the
backyard, and a young hockey star named Stu MacLure who
would occasionally play with me. My older-by-a-year-sister
Bernadine and I played together in our apartment. One morning, I woke up to find my younger brother silent, dark, and cold,
and my mother and father crying. My first close encounter with
death.

A few months later, we moved to Sydney Street in
Charlottetown's west end—halfway down the block heading
to Connaught Square. Connaught Square was a great place
because it provided ample place to play—especially baseball—
in the summer. There were plenty of kids in that area of the city,
which had more than its share of baseball players of all ages.
The baseball stars in the city at that time included names like
the Whitlocks, MacNeills, Stanleys, LeClairs, Pineaus, Ryans,
and others. We lived in a big apartment building on Sydney
Street. Within a year or two, the building and the rest of the
block were sold to make room for the Dominion Building, now
the home of Cox & Palmer law firm.

● ● ●

Dad—James Leslie MacDonald—was born on August 10, 1912, in Peakes Station in Kings County, PEI. His parents were Ronnie Dan and Tillie, who gave him four brothers and five sisters. Earl, who was also a top player with Peakes' baseball teams, operated the mixed farm in Peakes until the late 1950s when he moved to Boston where the money was much better than in farming. His other brothers were Leonard, who lived in Charlottetown, David, and Chester who later moved to the USA. Dad's older sister Granville moved to Boston; Etta (McQuaid) lived in the Peakes area; Aunt Bernadine was a favorite of ours because she always sent money at Christmas time; Aunt Marian lived in Maine; but Dad was closest with his sister Georgie Affleck, who taught school at St Jean's for many years. Aunt Georgie's sons—Les, Dennis, and Brian—were all prominent athletes in Charlottetown.

The MacDonald women played together in a band in the Peakes-St. Theresa-Pisquid area. I suppose this is where Dad learned to play the fiddle, where he earned the nickname "Fiddler" or "Jimmy Fiddler." In the early 1930s, he moved to Charlottetown to attend St. Dunstan's University from approximately 1932 to 1936. He graduated at 24 years old in 1936 with a Bachelor of Arts degree in commerce.[1] During his years at SDU, he was very active in several sports including varsity rugby, basketball, hockey, and track and field. In a 1952 article in *The Guardian*, Father Walter McGuigan, who was the athletic director at SDU, named Dad as one of the top rugby players he had ever coached. He was more than an excellent athlete during his student days; Dad was also co-editor of the *Red and White Review*, which covered the university scene.

Fiddler didn't talk very much about his exploits on the baseball diamonds, the rugby fields, or at St. Dunstan's, but I often

1935 SDU Rugby team. Father Walter McGuigan who served a role similar to today's athletic director sits for the team photo.

Jimmy Fiddler MacDonald, the SDU Rugby captain, holds the rugby ball.

SDU Graduation Class 1936, Fiddler, top row, far right.

heard about his activities from regulars at Connaught Square like Alkie MacCormack or Elmer MacNeill. Years later, when I started to do assignments for school, I realized that Dad was a very bright and well-read man, who knew far more about world affairs than many on PEI. Much later, he demonstrated his writing skills in major articles on the beginnings of PEI baseball for *The Guardian's* 1873–1973 100th anniversary issue. He was a man of many talents.

Dad wasn't outgoing and he didn't say very much about his pitching days with PEI-based teams, although "when he had a few aboard," he would often talk about other Peakes' standouts like his brother Earl or catcher George Smith who played university ball in Boston. In fact, I later learned that he had been a terrific baseball pitcher in the province: he struck out

24 of 27 batters against an all-star team from Charlottetown, on July 12, 1936, while he was with Peakes' baseball team. That feat brought him much notoriety. That game was played in Charlottetown. Below is the box-score:

Sunday, July 12, 1936: Peakes 7, Charlottetown 2

Charlottetown All-stars 2 runs, 2 hits, 2 errors

PLAYER	POSITION	AT BATS	RUNS	HITS
Tic Williams	2nd base	3	1	1
Joe MacDougall	Short Stop	4	0	0
Chevy Acorn	Left Field	4	1	2
Fred Bradly	Centre Field	4	0	0
Hector McQuarrie	Left Base	2	0	0
Bill McCallum	3rd Base	4	0	0
Elmer Larter	Pitcher	2	0	0
I. McLeod	Right Field	3	0	0
Vern Larter	Catcher	3	0	0

Peakes 7 runs, 10 hits, 2 errors

PLAYER	POSITION	AT BATS	RUNS	HITS
J. Curran	2nd Base	4	2	1
J. Mooney	Left Field	5	0	2
G. Smith	Catcher	4	0	0
E. MacDonald	Short Stop	4	2	2
B. Connolly	Centre Field	4	0	1
J. MacDonald	Pitcher	3	2	1
K. Mooney	3rd Base	5	0	1
E. Smith	1st base	5	1	2
L. MacDonald	Centre Field	5	0	0

After university, Dad moved to Amherst, NS, to pitch for the Amherst St. Pats from 1937 to 1938 against the top mainland teams like Springhill and Halifax. Many years later, he received a letter from a former teammate. Bill Kiley, who played professional baseball in the United States in the mid-1930s with the St Louis Browns' organization, wrote Dad in the 1980s. The letter gives insight into the type of pitcher Fiddler had been prior to the Second World War:

> Well Fiddler, in my day I caught the best in the Maritimes like Johnny Harvey here in Saint John and Charlie Nichols in Minto who was by the way south with Cincinnati and was farmed out after spring training...when asked like I was this past summer who was the best pitcher I ever taught, without hesitation I said Fiddler MacDonald. Most people here in Saint John didn't know about you but I sure did. [Bill Kiley, Saint John, New Brunswick 1982]

Unfortunately, Fiddler had little time to enjoy the fun of playing baseball or of exploring opportunities that might have come his way as the Second World War broke out in September 1939. Dad enlisted almost immediately on September 16 in Dartmouth with the Prince Edward Island Highlanders D Company. Like most veterans, he didn't say much about the war, but his attestation/military papers and health records reveal some details. On November 11, he was promoted to Corporal. On June 20, 1940, he was promoted to Sergeant. Between 1939 and 1942, he was stationed with the PEI Highlanders in Halifax, NS, Valcartier, QC, Botwood and Gander, NL, and Long Branch and Brandon, ON. He also spent some time in a military hospital in December 1942.

In 1943, Dad's moves took him from Brandon for the Anti-Tank Qualifying course (January 4), to Saint John, NB, to the Canadian Infantry Training Centre for the Officers' Refresher course (June 19), where, on August 6, he was promoted to Lieutenant. On November 4, Dad was in Prince George, BC, for the second Anti-Tank Battle Wing course, returning to his unit on December 12, 1943. On January 24, 1944, he returned to BC for the Mountain Warfare course, returning to his unit sometime in February. The Canadian Armed Forces (CAF) must have seen something special in Fiddler to have invested so much time in his training.

Dad obviously also had time for courting and a honeymoon. He married Mom, Mary Geraldine "Patricia" Bradley of St. Theresa on April 17, 1944, returning to his unit on May 3. He left for Britain on December 19 and the war in Europe, disembarking on December 25. Unfortunately, he was not at home for the birth of his and Pat's first child, Helen Bernadine, on January 23, 1945.

He was in the UK until February 12, 1945, when he was flown to Europe. On March 17, Fiddler was taken on strength with the North Nova Scotia Highlanders (NNSH or North Novies) and served as Anti-Tank Platoon Commander. The North Novies were involved in the Rhine Crossing operation, which began on March 23. The NNSH and 9th Canadian Brigade were part of the force that was expanding the bridgehead down river towards the Dutch border and into Germany. On March 25, NNSH and Dad came on during the night to take Bienen, Germany. The fighting was fierce—the second-worse day of losses for the NNSH during the whole war.[2]

Dad was hit in the right shoulder and the right leg, causing a compound fracture of his leg. He was evacuated to the UK and the 4th Canadian Hospital for treatment where he spent many months recovering and rehabilitating before returning to Canada. He was honourably discharged on October 23, 1945, "being unable to meet the required military physical standards." For his service in Canada, Newfoundland, Britain, Belgium, Holland, and Germany, Dad was given the 1939-45 Star, the France and Germany Star, the Defence Medal, the Canadian Volunteer Service Medal with Clasp, and the War Medal 1939–45.[3]

After the war, Dad taught upgrading to veterans at the Prince of Wales College and, when that ended in 1950, worked at various jobs until finding full-time employment with Canada Post until his retirement. Because of his war-time injuries, Dad wasn't able to pursue a career in professional baseball, so he volunteered his time as a senior baseball coach in Charlottetown and brought me along as batboy along with Wally McInnis and Jamie Kennedy, who became my life-long friends.

Raising a young, growing family in Charlottetown at this time was a struggle especially on the meagre wage that Dad earned. How young and growing? Well, Bernadine was born in 1945; I was born August 15, 1946; Ian (Tex) was born July 27, 1947; Ramona on June 5, 1949; then came Urban (Rabs), Alexander (Sandy), Hubert (Sock), Bonnie, Gary (Sput), Margaret (Peggy), Jamie-Ellen, Scott (1962); and Monica (?). I honestly can't say most of the actual birthdays, but I do know that Tex and I are "Irish twins"—the same age for three weeks between July 27 and August 15.

Mom was always pushing Dad to look for various jobs that were more suited to his talents, abilities, and education. In those days, few adults and even fewer veterans had a university degree, and Dad's reluctance to pursue better jobs, despite his education, was often a source of argument between the two when they were seated at the kitchen table. Mom found it a struggle to pay the bills and she often wondered why some veterans received a cheque, but Fiddler did not. She talked to family friend Jim Hogan who did plenty of work on behalf of veterans and it wasn't until the late 1950s or early 1960s that Dad received monetary help: a pension for his service in the Second World War.

Mom was about 5'2" and 120 pounds. She was assertive and always on the go. Her mother, Margaret Hughes, was born and mostly lived in St. Theresa, a few miles up the road from Peakes. She had been a schoolteacher in New York City, where Mom was born on October 5, 1924. Mom had three sisters—Peggy (Bradley) Rothermel, Hudson, Ohio; Helen (Bradley) Verner, Euclid, Ohio; Marcy (Bradley) Zelazny, Birmingham, Michigan; and four brothers—Leo Bradley, Ottawa; John Bradley, Peakes; Urban Bradley, Germany; and Jimmy Bradley, Toronto. Mom and her sisters graduated from the Souris Convent, and, just as her mother had insisted on strong schooling, Mom followed with a similar plan for her kids—us. She insisted that each of us be given the opportunity to receive a university education.

One of the aspects of raising a large family that Mom liked the most was attending all of the parent-teacher interviews. She got to know every teacher in Charlottetown, and they knew her on a very personal basis. She had their phone numbers and did not hesitate to call if she detected something not quite right with the schooling. She never had any problems with my reports, but I can't say that's true for all the boys and girls.

Before Monica, the final child, was sent off to school in the 1970s, Mom had upgraded her skills at night school in the hopes of finding employment in the city. She wanted to be out of the house after decades of raising kids, to enjoy her own money, and soon landed a job in the Land Registry office. She stayed there until her retirement. She had always wanted to visit her Bradley family roots in Ireland, and when Monica graduated from the University of Edinburgh, Scotland, Mom told us that this was her chance to visit Dublin. Despite the size of our family, Mom always helped family members in need either financially or with baby sitting. She stayed that way right to the end.

Sydney Street was an ideal location for young growing families as both the school and the church were within a quarter-mile, as well the near-by farmers' market in Market Square on Queen Street. My younger brother Ian and I went there daily for goodies such as fudge, brownies, and a wide assortment of baked and grown items. We learned our first important lesson there: if we looked poor, we were more apt to be rewarded with an assortment of free goodies. As well, Queen Square School, a Catholic-only boys' school, was a couple hundred yards away. Of

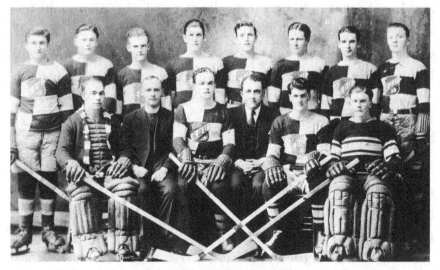

St. Dunstan's University hockey team, 1936. Fiddler is in second row, fourth from the right.

course, St. Dunstan's Basilica was and still is a prominent struc-
ture on the corner of Sydney and Great George Streets.

In those days, baseball was the most popular summertime
game, not just in the city but also across the Island from Tignish
to Souris. There was no shortage of top players. It was the game
for the masses and although rugby, track and field, and cycling
were very popular, the majority of young boys played baseball
in the summer and hockey in the winter. A few kids in the city,
whose parents came over from England after the Second World
War, kicked around a soccer ball, but few boys knew anything
about the game or even knew what a soccer ball was. Paul
Taylor was the first youngster to kick a soccer ball at the Holy
Redeemer Field located where St. Jean School is today, but the
ball disappeared, and nothing became of the game at that time.

When *The Guardian* newspaper printed its 100th anniversary
edition, Lou Campbell was regarded as one of PEI's top athletes
in our first 100 years. George "Shauna" Francis was not only a top
catcher with the Madisons but he also later played a major role
in baseball development in the city over the next fifty years. Also
with the Madisons was Manager Dr. Charles Dougan, who was a
prominent organizer in all sports in the City and harness racing's
most colorful starter until his passing in the early 1950s.

By the early 1950s, Fiddler could no longer play baseball,
but he spent much of his spare time at the baseball park. Family
responsibilities rested with our mother Pat or, as she was called,
Pat Fiddler. These were times of great fun at the ball park but,
as mentioned above, raising a large family can put a lot of stress
on any relationship.

Dad coached in the highly popular City Baseball League
and took his team, the Maritime Central Airways-sponsored
Flyers, to the 1953 Maritime Championship Intermediate A

Crown with three outstanding left-handed pitchers in Lefty McAleer, Jack "Poochie" Burke, and Waldo Munroe, who was the piano player for the famous PEI and Maritime band Don Messier and the Islanders.

The 1955 Charlottetown Flyers, a shortened version of the sponsor Carl Burke's Maritime Central Airways Flyers, captured the city regular season crown: The team included Brian Lewis, Elmer MacNeill, Bernie Gallant, Fiddler MacDonald, Don Funnel MacLean, Ron Stanley, Kip Ready, Merlin Devine, Bobby Lund, Cuker Pineau, Jack Kane, and Jack Burke.

The 1956 Charlottetown team won the Maritime Intermediate A Crown beating the Memramcook Rovers two games to one. Fiddler and Tom MacFarlane, another top coach, handled the team. The team picture had such notables as coach Tom MacFarlane, Jack "Spy" Ready, Vern Handrahan who went on to pitch with the Oakland As in 1961, Kip Ready, Don Funnell MacLean, Irv MacKinnon, Charlie Ryan and Roy "Buck" Whitlock, Jack Burke, Ken MacDonald, Frank "Doughboy" Shepherd, Cuker Pineau, batboy, Fred MacDonald, Bob Lund, Jack Kane, and Fiddler MacDonald.

By 1956, Fiddler was enjoying great success coaching baseball, and his experience with and knowledge of the game proved to be great assets. Fiddler knew how to speak to people in a respectful manner, always considering another person's point of view. As a student of the baseball game, and as a player at the highest levels in the Maritimes, he made an ideal coach. Since Tex and I had started playing minor ball in the city, the fun had just begun. With Dad coaching and a few of the boys in minor leagues, the MacDonald family was making its name in the city's sporting community.

CHAPTER 2

Queen Square vs. Queen Charlotte

THE QUEEN SQUARE SCHOOL—THE ALL-BOYS
Catholic school located on the corner lot of Richmond and
Great George, across the street from the Basilica Church in the
centre of the city—was dramatically different from the school
systems of today. No such thing as integrated classes. The girls
attended Notre Dame Academy. School started at 8:30AM and
classes ended with the 3:00PM bell. Many of the male teachers
were St. Dunstan's graduates who encouraged the students from
an early age to support and attend games at Holy Name Hall,
later the Basilica Rec Centre, and advised Queen Square boys
not to attend functions at the YMCA. That was out of bounds
because Catholic students were instructed never to attend
Protestant gatherings.

Since everyone who attended Queen Square was mandated
to attend the Basilica, the church was usually packed on Holy
Days and especially on Sunday. The legendary Reverend Patrick
McMahon, D.D., better known as Father Pat, often delivered
sermons that would "tell about visits from the devil." He was
a powerful speaker and, with his face flushed red, his shaking
and crying from the pulpit, it seemed like the finger of God
pointed at us.

We often wondered what the folks who attended other churches did. There was no chance of going to visit The Kirk or the St. Peter's Anglican or any other of the non-Catholic churches in the city. The only other church we were allowed to attend was the Holy Redeemer where St. Jean School is today. The other churches were taboo or out of bounds for anybody at Queen Square, as if there were something sinister about those places.

From grade one, the animosity towards the other Protestant schools came to the forefront in the athletic competitions, especially in rugby and hockey. It was a rivalry that began back at the turn of the century. In 1928, to help promote rugby in the city schools, and possibly to promote attendance at both St. Dunstan's and Prince of Wales College, an interscholastic championship began. West Kent and Queen Square schools took turns winning for extended periods of time. The competition was withdrawn in 1938 due to the hostility between West Kent and Queen Square students and their parents.

Organizers must have felt that the time was ripe to renew the rugby rivalry, and in 1956, the City Schools Rugby championship was rekindled with Queen Square edging Queen Charlotte in a best of five series that was bitterly contested. I fondly remember attending one of those games with my brother Tex, which took place behind Queen Charlotte school. In that 1956 game, Jim MacCallum's Queen Square team dumped Queen Charlotte, and eventually won that best of five series.

In the fall of 1957, late October—early November, the city title was again on the line. In this one, Queen Charlotte upset Queen Square for the championship. The games were played at Memorial Field and behind Queen Charlotte, and drew huge crowds as rugby attracted a large following in the province and in the Maritimes. A sizeable contingent of students from Queen Square watched the final game played on the field just off North River Road. The fans included not only boys from Queen Square and Queen Charlotte, but also those who attended St. Dunstan's and PWC, as well as those who had played back in 1928.

This game had many sub-plots: not only was it the Catholics vs the Protestants, it featured Jack "Spy" Ready coaching previous rival Queen Charlotte against Queen Square. Spy had put together a rugged club and they took the title from Bill Ledwell and Fred Driscoll's Queen Square boys club in an exciting game. I heard in many quarters that Spy should be ex-communicated for handling the Queen Charlotte club. Not in our house, because Mom and Dad loved Spy; he had pitched for Dad's baseball team, was a personable guy, and a close family friend.

1949—Charlottetown Senior team—Ch'town Anchors
Back Row: left to right: Lem Rush, Fiddler, Harold Gaudet, Hector MacQuarrie,
Earl Nicholson, Dinty Stanley; Front Row: Jim Flanagan, Willie MacTague, Frank Steele,
Ivan "Fats" Connors, Mike Hennessey, Bat boy—Leroy MacDonald

I still remember the game as if it was yesterday. Queen Charlotte had guys like Roy Scantlebury, David Ives, Cox, Lea, MacPherson, Matensin, John Curtis, Roger MacDonald, Oscar Mallett; halves: Billy MacMillan (captain), David Rogers, Don MacAusland, Don Kelly, Alan Brady, Fred Curtis, and Don Frizzell; fullback, Stu MacFadyen. Queen Square: forwards: Mickey Peters, Brian Morris, Oodie Hayes, Beaver Arsenault, Ron MacKinnon, Colin MacMillan; halves: Frank Callaghan, Ron MacDougall, Ray Malone, Leonard Stull, Emmett Beagan, Fred Burke, Steve Connolly; fullback: Alan MacDonald.

Once the rugby season ended, the rivalry didn't, carrying over into minor hockey league and into the school system, especially when Prince Street, West Kent, or Queen Charlotte were matched against Queen Square. The annual school ice sports games were the climax of the year for Queen Square kids as the games were played out of the old Charlottetown Forum on Fitzroy Street. By 1958, the last year that Queen Square staged its ice sports, they won the Archer Trophy for the second year in a row defeating arch rivals Queen Charlotte 7-3 as Fred Burke, Alf Flanagan, and Wayne MacDonald proved too much for Bill MacMillan, David Rogers, and company.

That same year, our family moved from Sydney Street to 26 Spring Street between Churchill Avenue and Villa Street. What a wonderful upbringing we had. There were so many kids on the go: the MacGillivray family, the Byers family, the Wayes, the Shepherds—star softball players Paddy and Wilf Shepherd—the MacLures, the Durants on Villa, the Davies on Churchill, the Hennesseys on Churchill, and on Peake and Euston streets, the Toombs boys, the Hartingers, the MacLeans, Mousie Hughes, and the O'Donnells, with the famous lawyer, Lester. One of my life-long friends Wally McInnis came to our house every day as we all headed to the ballpark, Wally coming from Bayfield along with Piper and some of his brothers.

We had a big pond in our backyard, which also served as a ball park in the summer months. There was another unofficial ball park on the corner lot where Churchill intersected Peake, and between these two "parks" and Memorial Field, there was little else to do. The move to Spring Street gave us a chance to experience harness racing first hand.

When we lived on Sydney Street, the Noonans lived directly across the street. Gerald Noonan was just starting as a trainer-driver. His colours were blue and white, and during the 1957 summer harness racing season, my father and I visited the Charlottetown Driving Park when Gerald was making his driving debut. He drove a horse that day called Josedale Courier and they won. It was the beginning of my lifelong love of harness racing. On our move to Spring Street, we got an even bigger taste of harness racing. In those days, horsemen were allowed to keep their horses at home just as you would a pet. Maurice Hennessey's barn on Churchill Avenue bordered on the backyard and Fred Dalziel had horses that bordered the yard facing Peake Street. Maurice would get annoyed when sometimes a baseball shattered his barn window; he was a good guy and eventually put wire over the window to prevent any future breaking.

Joe Hennessey lived at the top of the lane on Euston and Peake streets. It's no longer a street, but during this time, "the lane" represented the race track. Horses were matched for races from the head of the lane to Churchill Avenue. Strings made of baler twine were fashioned to make driving reins, and switches from Victoria Park became the whips.

Wally McInnis drove me, Jody Hennessey drove Tex, Wendell Toombs drove Eddy, Willie McInnis, father of fiddler Bill, drove Eddy Hartinger. We also drew for post positions. Wally McInnis used to cuff me a couple of hard ones to ensure I was running as fast as I could.

Joe Hennessey also had a barn on the Peake Street property where he stabled horses that raced at the city track. I recall four or five being there. In those days, Joe insisted that if we went in the barn to be very careful with certain horses. Joe made his living solely from training and racing, which was and still is a tough assignment in the Maritime provinces. We all got to appreciate the love for the horses at this early age, but there were other happenings that stayed in my mind. At the Hennessey household, even though they had a big family, a blind man named "John" stayed there permanently. We used to watch him work with the horses at the Hennessey barn. One of the horses was a bad-tempered, bad-acting horse called Cheeky Chief that we were to avoid. He would run at us with his teeth bared but once John came into the barn, his temperament would change dramatically. John would take him out of the stall, put him on the lines, clean him, and do his feet, and he'd act like the most beautiful animal one could ever see. Nevertheless, we took Joe's advice and never entered that stall.

On the days it rained, we sometimes staged boxing matches in the stalls if there was one empty. Jody was the match-maker and judge, and he would close the stall door and the bout would begin. The rounds lasted two minutes or until the blood started running. I remember one such match when Harry Yeo challenged Tex, which was a mistake for Harry. Tex battered Harry from one side of the stall to the other. Judge Jody should have stopped the fight long before.

CHAPTER 3

Hot Off The Press:
The News Boys

THERE WERE ALWAYS PLENTY OF WAYS TO MAKE SOME
money in our spare time in those days and by 1958, selling
newspapers, shining shoes, or selling worms were all money
makers. Whatever it took, I did it. The newspaper business
was especially lucrative, not so much the sale of *The Guardian*,
but the afternoon city paper, *The Evening Patriot*. Since Queen
Square was right next to where the *Patriot* was printed on
Sydney Street, the afternoon Charlottetown newspaper was
easy to sell. It contained all the news that had happened the
previous night especially the late baseball and hockey scores.
I couldn't wait for school to finish as I had a *Patriot* route of
regular customers, plus the street sales. I bought the newspaper
right off the press for one cent each and sold them for three
cents plus tips.

By 3:15PM, I would have picked up my papers at the *Patriot*
plant on Sydney Street and turned at the corner to head up
Queen Street to hit all the hot spots in the middle of the city.

My first stop was Prowse Brothers Ltd. merchants on the
corner of Queen and Richmond. Every day, William Prowse,
who was PEI's Lieutenant Governor from 1950 to 1958 (therefore during my paper-selling days), would buy a paper from me,
hand me a "Pontiac nickel," and wait for his two cents change.

Every day my answer would be the same: "Sir, you are my first customer and I have no change." He would reply, "Go next door to Reddin Pharmacy and take me back the change." This routine went on for five or six years and, after a while, it became a test as to who would bend first.

Craswell's Studio on Great George St.
Fred Lambros Store on the corner of Kent and Great George.

Market Square was always a hot spot for sales, and being the first *Patriot* seller there usually resulted in high sales: 10 or so papers in a jiffy. Directly across from the Market Square on Queen was Woolworths Five and Ten store. Next to it and extending to the corner was Rogers Hardware. The Five and Ten had a long counter shaped like a seven with seats where people liked to sit and read the paper. I learned to be at the Rogers corner at 3:45PM to 4:00PM as some of my best customers approached that area as supper time beckoned. I don't know whether the bootleggers closed for supper, but I got to know some of them. They were my best tippers. One of my top customers at that corner was Pete Campbell, one of the bootlegger's part-time clients.

Heading over to the next block and up Queen Street, there were restaurants on one side, Dominion Grocery Store, Toombs' Music, and Jimmy Power's shoeshine stand, but they sold their own papers so I didn't go in there. The chap that ran the store for Jimmy was John Lane, an extremely bright young man who later became a high-ranking officer in the Armed Forces. I believe he was enrolled in the Royal Officers Training Program and he was one smart cookie. He was a big Baltimore Orioles fan. He would listen to the ball games on the radio and, after a hit, he would deliver the hitter's new batting average within seconds. On Friday nights when the boys from the country came to town, Lane hired me and two of my close boyhood friends Wayne MacDougall and Jamie Kennedy to shine shoes.

The next block featured Ment's Restaurant and further down on the corner of Fitzroy and Queen was ABC Cutcliffe Funeral Home. One of my favourite customers was upstairs on the third floor of the Queen Street side of Cutcliffe's: Les Alexander who played with Don Messier and the Islanders. He always tipped me and I made sure not to be late with his paper.

My route then took me down Fitzroy, heading to the corner where the Irish bar, The Triangle is today. In my paperboy days, Garden City Dairy operated out of there. They made some of the best ice cream in the city. It was not a great place to sell newspapers because it had no space, so I would head back up Great George to Kent Street where I would stop at Craswell's Photo Shop and Gallery. Cleve and his wife Babe were the finest people a paperboy would ever meet.

After Cleve passed away, the Bike Shop took over the Craswell Studio but the memories from Cleve and his wife stay close to my heart. Everyday I went to the studio, Babe would take me out back, sit me down, and she'd have a glass of milk and a couple of cookies for me. She'd ask me how the day was going, how the brothers and sisters were, and how many papers I had sold. They always gave me more than they should have but I wasn't complaining. My first Christmas as their paper boy, the Craswells had a big parcel for me, not to be opened until Christmas day. A new pair of pants, and a new sweater and shirt was a mighty big gift in those days. My mother always said to pray for them and I always did, believing all along those non-Catholics were not going where we were going after finishing our time on earth.

After leaving Craswell's studio, I headed across the street to Fred Lambrose's store on the corner of Great George and Kent where Financial Services is today. Fred had a shoeshine stand there and he also sold papers, so my appearance there was a short one. There were always characters there, guys like Harry "The Barber" Sentner, and some of the local sports stars.

The Lambrose Store had two entrances, one on the corner straddling Great George and Kent, and the other on the Kent Street side. Directly across the street was the Milton's Old Spain Tea Room, which later became known as Myron's. All the big hockey players of the day went there, but Mrs. Bell was strictly business and she didn't want paper boys bothering the customers, although Myron looked the other way.

Up on the next corner, Johnny's Mayfair owned and operated by Johnny Squarebriggs was always a going concern. They had a circular counter restaurant with great meals, run by my sister-in-law, Anita's mom Theresa. Johnny's Mayfair sold more sports newspapers, especially the *Sporting News,* than anywhere in the city: it was the favorite hangout for the many baseball and hockey standouts. Johnny would start a conversation and soon the arguments would begin, whatever sport you wanted to talk about: hockey, curling, track, baseball, or harness racing, Johnny had the answers and usually he was right on. Oh, the arguments in there with Pius Callaghan, Duck Acorn, Vic MacDonald, Chris Gallant, Doug Cameron, Richard Bradley, and others.

My best friend, Wally, also had his own paper route. When we finished with the Patriots, we'd also sell the *Halifax Herald* for Ivan Monaghan, who was the distribution manager. Sometimes Wally had to be at the track helping his uncle on race days. On those days, I took along my brother Sandy to educate him on the newspaper business. Ivan's office was between Ment's Restaurant and the fire hall entrance on Queen Street. We always picked up the papers at around 4:30PM, since we had to be home for supper at 6:00PM, we had to be fast. Wally and I would split the papers—25 each—and head for the waterfront at the bottom of Queen and Prince. That's where the big ships, like the *Tupper* and the *Sorel*, would dock. I can remember selling the *Halifax Herald* at the docks a few years later. Some of the boats had come from Cuba and showed bullet marks and shell hits, which the crew members said were from the 1961 Bay of Pigs Invasion in Cuba.

By the winter of 1958, I got my first pair of skates from Gerry Kane who lived on Queen Street across from the Telephone Company, and halfway between Euston and Fitzroy. My brother Tex also got his first pair of skates from the Garden City Dairy guys who delivered milk to our place on Spring Street by horse and wagon. Tex had struck up a relationship with the two drivers Leith Carr and Kenny Ford, who later was better known in US harness racing circles (especially Sportsman's Park, Chicago), as Lou Forbes or Shakey Louie. They dropped off an army duffle bag with the name Garrison Juniors on it. In the bag were skates and gear that Tex used for many years.

Kenny Ford loved harness racing and left Charlottetown in the mid-1960s and found employment immediately as a caretaker in the States. He worked for several years with the great driver Buddy Gilmour, and later as a caretaker for train-er-driver Robert Farrington out of Chicago. Kenny, or Shakey Louie, went on to become one of the most colourful characters in the harness racing world. Farrington and owner Lloyd Arnold of the Arnold Cattle Company were major players on the US harness racing scene as the stable campaigned the 1969 Maple Leaf Trot winner, Grandpa Jim. He also worked for Jim Dennis and looked after such great horses like Sir Dalrae and

Try Scotch. Kenny became great friends with Chicago Hockey coach Billy Ray and Jim Pappin, and players John Ferguson and Serge Savard, who were in the race game back in the late 1960s in Montreal. Kenny worked at the winners' circle at Chicago harness racing tracks until his passing in 2010.

As for minor hockey, it was a lot of fun, but there was plenty of enjoyment at the government pond, which was a short walk from our house on Spring Street to just off Euston Street. Gerry Kane taught me how to play hockey. He was almost two years older than me and in 1960, he moved me onto the top line with himself and Pete Pineau on the Queen Square Foxes. I was among the league's top scorers in a division that included Bill Weatherbie, Lloyd Blanchard, Harvey Cormier, Freddie Roberts, Bob Peterson, and Model School stars Jamie Kennedy

1956 Maritime Champions Charlottetown Intermediate
Back Row: Coach Tom MacFarlane, Spy Ready, Vern Handrahan, Kip Ready,
Don MacLean, Irv MacKinnon, Charlie Ryan, Buck Whitlock; Front Row: Jack Poochie
Burke, Ken MacDonald, Frank "Doughboy" Shepherd, Cuker Pineau, bat-boy Fred
Fiddler MacDonald, Bobby Lund, Jack Kane, coach Fiddler MacDonald.

and George Shorty MacDonald. I felt bad about this because Gerry wasn't close friends with Billy Weatherbie, and Gerry didn't allow him to play on the first line over me. He should have. Billy was probably the next best player at that age in the city other than Gerry. The following year, Gerry graduated to Bantam A. I was demoted to the AA team under Dr. Theriault with my first-line pals Lloyd Blanchard and Harvey Cormier.

CHAPTER 4

Take Us Out To The Ball Games

MOST OF US LOOKED FORWARD TO THE SUMMER AND the baseball season, and we usually got a head start by playing on the kite field just up from the government pond and on the open field in front of the Prince Edward Island Hospital. That field dried up quicker than anywhere else and it became our spring training camp. The summer of 1958, I decided to try pitching as I was a little stronger. Tex and I had developed strong, rifle arms throwing in the backyard against a barn trying to strike out the brothers with a tennis ball from 40 paces. We would burn the hair off a tennis ball so that the seams were exposed; throwing across the seams made the ball rise and would sink the ball. Tex often threw at me, hitting me with a bullet on the ass or on the shoulder. Naturally, I would return the trick. In time, Urban (Rabs), Gary (Sput), Hubert (Sockie), Alexander (Sandy), and Scott followed in the game. Doing that every day, no wonder fastballs didn't get past us or our brothers who were exposed to the same training so young.

During the summer, the backyard at Spring Street became a training camp of sorts for up-and-coming pitchers, especially in the City Senior League. Fiddler had built a baseball mound, and here is where right-handed pitcher Handrahan came to polish his skills in holding men on base and handling himself on the mound.

Vern talked to Bill Ledwell in a 1974 interview:

Fiddler and Tom MacFarlane, my first real coaches, taught me how to stand on the mound, concentrate on the hitter, and hold runners on first. Fiddler spent a lot of time teaching me how to throw the curve. We used to spend hours in Fiddler's backyard on Spring Street, and I learned the basics there.

Vern went on to pitch with the Oakland As in the late 1960s playing with legends like Reggie Jackson, Sal Bando, Vida Blue, Joe Rudi, and many others. Vern pitched against Mickey Mantle and Roger Maris at Yankee Stadium. That is a long way from Spring Street in Charlottetown.

The backyard baseball games usually included Wally McInnis, Tex, Rabs, Willie McInnis, George Curley, Ian Waye, Ernie Davey, Jackie Durant, Eddy and Wendell Tombs, Ed Hartinger, Sock, Sandy, some of the Hennessey boys, and Bill and Winston Weatherbie who lived just over the back fence on the corner of Spring Park Road and Victory Avenue. When not at Victoria Park, the vacant lot on Churchill Avenue and Peake, or our backyard, served as the ball park. In the fall, the same cast usually showed up on the Kite Field just below the Prince Edward Hospital. Sometimes the sisters played.

My sister Bernadine loved music and was a talented piano player. She had no time for such foolishness as football, but Ramona played and enjoyed it. In fact, in the draft of players the boys would often draft Ramona over Rabbit because she could run fast. In her teens, she was a sprinter in track and field. She would just as soon run over you than around you. Rabbit was smaller and lighter, and he didn't mind being overlooked in the draft as he firmly believed that he could beat anyone at any game including football.

As one would expect with a very large family, money was sometimes scarce, but not for me or Wally. We had a booming summer-time shoe-shine business, which we operated in the city centre just beyond the Henderson and Cudmore doors. Since we worked occasionally shining shoes at the Jim Powers' stand, we knew there was money to be made. Wally and I would shine only after the papers had been sold. Saturdays in July and August were great for business: if the weather was good and the tourists were around, we might stay all day. I looked after the money. Wally sometimes asked just how I arrived at the 50-50 split: "Take your expenses out first, then we split." That's my story and I'm sticking to it. It's the same formula I used with younger brother Sandy when we sold papers or when he helped with the shoe shine business. He still questions my math.

In the summer evenings, most kids that lived near the park watched the City Baseball League in action. Everyone had a personal hero. The League had developed top players such as pitchers Vern Handrahan, Buck Whitlock, Lefty McAleer, Roger MacLeod, Jack Burke, young George "Lefty" Dunn, and Don Funnel MacLean; catchers Forbie Kennedy and Arnold MacCallum; infielders Jack Kane, Bobby Lund, Lorne Hennessey, Joey LeClair, Cuker Pineau, Say Doiron, Bobby Rice, slugger Elmer MacNeil, and so many more.

Another standout was Don "Duck" MacLeod who would later pitch pro with the World Series champion Milwaukee Braves organization, which was stacked with pitchers Lou Burdette,

Warren Spahn, Bob Buhl, Juan Pizarro, and Joey Jay. They reduced Duck's chances for a major league breakthrough.

By the summer of 1959, I had grown a little bigger and had the opportunity to learn some things about pitching from Fiddler in the backyard. It was during the 1959-60 era that Bobby Lund organized the baseball teams in a revolutionary way. Minor hockey and the teams under Brig Reid and Al Rodgers were organized by schools such as the Queen Square Foxes, the Queen Charlotte Lions, and the Prince Street Falcons. Therefore, we didn't get the chance to play with boys outside of Queen Square or Birchwood. Bobby Lund put the teams together, trying to balance the teams regardless of which schools they had attended the previous winter. I got to play with guys including Jamie Kennedy, Robert MacNutt, Brian Munroe, Ron Boyles, Paul Michael, John Irwin, Tuppy Rogers, Chick MacCallum, Wayne MacDougall, Robert Taylor, Ron Diamond, Ginger Breedon, and Lyle Huggan. Jamie, of course, has been one of my great lifetime friends.

As a pitcher, I also enjoyed some success. Ian Purvis was an outstanding pitcher and the dominant player in the little league ranks at that time, and Billy Weatherbie was another top player. The teams played nine or ten games every two weeks plus practice. Additionally, some of us played up in Taylor's Field beyond North River Road—normally out of bounds for Queen Square boys.

It was a breakout summer for me on the baseball diamond as we played for long hours every day, which benefited not only me but also several of our players. It showed down the road as the nucleus of this group won three or four Maritime Baseball titles in the Midget, Juvenile, and Junior ranks in the early 1960s.

Here's one of the headlines that appeared in *The Guardian* that summer:

"Young Fiddler Sets Up Record" (July 10, 1959)
Twelve-year-old Freddie MacDonald gave up a bunt single to Ron Boyles and a bloop single to Dave Soupy Campbell as the Little League Browns dumped the Dodgers 9-1 in Little League play yesterday at Memorial Field. The son of legendary Island pitcher Jimmy Fiddler MacDonald fanned 17 of 18 hitters for the victory. In other play, Robert MacNutt and Cyril MacDonald had three hits as the Giants downed the Red Sox.

Sportswriter Bill Ledwell's column "Like Father, Like Son" of Friday, July 10, 1959, wrote about this feat—the most strikeouts ever recorded in a Little League game to that time—in his daily column.

After Bobby Lund left for Dalhousie Medical School, Forbie Kennedy and Spy Ready ran the minor ball. The city eventually hired a full-time athletic director in Jim Fox, another top gentleman, still living in Moncton, New Brunswick. Bobby's foresight at establishing baseball teams among all players regardless of what school they attended broke down many barriers and proved to be one of the best decisions taken in city athletics. I thought of this ten years later when politicians and others took credit for a transition and the amalgamation of Prince of Wales and St. Dunstan's into UPEI in 1969. The person who should have gotten much of the credit was Dr. Bobby Lund for breaking the barriers in religious discord.[4]

The Little League and Bantam teams under Bobby Lund played so many games that by the early 1960s, Charlottetown

Minor Baseball started to produce some excellent teams. The
1962 Charlottetown Abbies Midget team under coach Charlie
Ryan won the Maritime championship in Charlottetown in
straight games beating St. Stephen ace Billy Pierce at Memorial
Field before four-thousand fans. In those days, the grandstands
or bleachers extended far down the right and left field lines.
I had three hits in this game. Tex had four hits and made a
sensational catch in left field.

Right-hander Billy Weatherbie and lefty Carl McQuaid
handled the pitching chores while the infield was airtight with
Jamie Kennedy and Joe Gallant at second. Chick MacCallum
and Ginger Breedon were at first base while Billy Weatherbie
and I handled the left side of the diamond. Barry Ellis did
most of the catching while Wayne MacDougall played outfield

*Charlottetown Legion, Maritime Midget
Baseball Champion Abbies, 1962, brothers
Ian "Tex" and Fred "Fiddler" pose with
new Abbies Jackets.*

and did some catching. Ricky Gallant was another solid player who played first and outfield on what was the last Maritime Championship under the Abbies' banner.

The summer of 1963, the Charlottetown Legion took over the sponsorship under Charlie Ryan. Soon Mike Kelly and Walter Bradley joined our club. Both were terrific additions. Kelly was an outstanding pitcher and hitter, and Bradley a fiery little second baseman. Soon baseball fans packed Memorial Field. The Charlottetown Legionnaires added the Maritime Juvenile crown to their achievements as they looked next at the 1964 season.

Maritime champions Charlottetown Maritime Central Airways Flyers: Top Row (left to right) Elmer McNeill, Irv McKinnon, Des Trainor, Red MacKenzie, Earl MacKinnon, and Waldo Munroe; Front Row: Lefty McAleer, Brian Lewis, Lorne Hennessey, Paul Jay, Merlin Devine, and Jack Burke. (Missing Coach Fiddler MacDonald, Don "Duck" MacLeod and Arnold MacCallum.)

Sports fans often read about and witness hockey fights involving just about every player on either team. It also happens in football and basketball, but seldom is such behavior seen in baseball games. In the Maritime 1963 Junior finals on the Halifax Commons, the Charlottetown Baseball Abbies, coached by Charlie Ryan with General Manager Charlie MacMillan, MP Tom MacMillan's older brother, faced the Halifax Cardinals in a sudden-death game for the Maritime title. The umpire for the game was RCMP officer Bill Coughlan.

Our coach Charlie was a Black Canadian. For those of us raised in Charlottetown, we didn't pay much attention to those who were darker-skinned. As my mother often said, they got more sun than us for a longer period. That sounded okay with me. I hadn't heard anything negative or racial in my life, but the Halifax crowd was throwing words at us that I had never heard before. I was playing third base and the Halifax dugout was close by: "Hey, you white boys playing for that black [so-and-so]?" It was hard to believe the language and the words they were using.

As the game progressed, we had the lead after four innings, and at the bottom of the fifth inning, Halifax threatened with the bases loaded. The ball was hit to me at third and my throw to the plate was high, but catcher Wayne MacDougall pulled it in and flattened the runner coming down the line. It was a heavy collision. Catcher MacDougall and Halifax's John Hanna traded punches. Umpire Coughlan tried as best he could to separate the two. Then the benches emptied and bats, gloves, rocks, and potatoes were thrown our way. The Ump called off the game fearing the safety of our coaches and players. Rocks hit our cars as we quickly gathered up our gear. Driver Roy White got us out of there, breaking speed records on the way to the ferry. Rather than forfeit the game and give us the title, the Maritime Baseball Association advised both teams that a sudden-death game would be played on neutral ground in Springhill, Nova Scotia, on October 29, 1963. We beat the Halifax Cardinals again, and claimed the last-ever championship baseball banner under the Charlottetown Abbies' name.

PEI's team at the 1965 National Junior championships in Winnipeg was a strong one. It should have been stronger; unfortunately, politics got in the way. Tex, who had hurt his shoulder playing football, was not on the team even though he was the best right-handed hitter in the province. In a crucial game at the Winnipeg tournament against Manitoba, we loaded the bases with none out against Winnipeg's ace lefty, who was

The Charlottetown Legion, 1962 Maritime Midget Baseball champions.
Front Row; left to right: Ian "Tex" MacDonald, Francis Lewis, batboy, Charlie Ryan,
Coach, Fred "Fiddler" MacDonald, Ricky Gallant; Middle Row: Jamie
Kennedy, Joe Gallant, Cy MacDonald, Barry Ellis, Billy Weatherbie, Carl McQuaid;
Back row, Wayne MacDougall, Lyle Huggan, Ginger Breedon, Chick
MacCallum, Posty Connolly, assistant coach.

engaged in a standout pitching duel with our Mike Kelly. Despite fourteen strike-outs in seven innings, Mike trailed 1-0. I felt hopeless standing on third base after a triple, and I could only imagine what Tex would have done against a fastball pitcher. We also had two other good right-handed hitters on the bench in George MacNeill and Paul MacWilliams.

In selecting the PEI team, there was always pressure on management to select so many from each county, so the best players didn't always made the team. Tex was as good a hitter as we had and he was left home; had we had Tex and used George MacNeill and Paul MacWilliams as pinch hitters with the bases loaded in that key game, I am certain the outcome would have been different. I learned early on that politics plays a major role in all aspects of PEI life.

After that tournament, four Charlottetown Legionnaires were selected to the Canadian National Junior Baseball Team for the international tournament in Mexico City: pitchers Mike Kelly and righty Bill Weatherbie, catcher Barry Ellis, and me in the infield.

Mike signed with the St. Louis Cardinals later that fall and he left in 1966 for the Rookie League. Weatherbie and I moved to Cape Cod in May; however, the league was a month away from opening and with no guarantees for work or play, we returned home. Our junior team disbanded. Tex moved to Montague with Jim MacDougall and took them to the Maritime finals. In 1967, I played with the Summerside Juniors and my friends, Paul MacWilliams, George MacNeill, Duck Gunning, and Doug MacDonald. We went to the Maritime finals losing in the last inning on a dropped fly ball to the outfield.

CHAPTER 5

The Scales Of Justice

BY 1967, WE HAD MOVED FROM SPRING STREET TO Moreau Drive, just off North River Road, and eventually to 87 Upper Prince Street, next to the Shaws, which is now where the Kanes live. The former principal at Queen Square and a family friend, J. Pius Callaghan, lived further down Prince Street. I needed a summer job, and J. Pius convinced me that I could do the job as *The Patriot* sports editor. I had done some work for him covering high school sports, and since Fiddler Sr. was an excellent writer, I had an exceptional resource person. The other aspect of the job that Pius asked me to do was to cover the City Police beat, which I knew nothing about. My godfather Leo MacDougall was an officer at the Police Station located on Kent Street, now where City Hall is.

In those days, *The Guardian* was still the morning paper, and for Charlottetown folks, *The Evening Patriot* was just as important especially on Saturday afternoons when the edition included the names of those who had been arrested on Friday nights. My awareness of justice and police work was confined to books of learning and watching television. I was just not prepared for the shock covering the City Police court.

On Saturday mornings at 7:30AM, I entered the Police Station, said hello to Sgt. Leo MacDougall, and talked for a few minutes about the night before. I hustled up to the second floor and the court house at City Hall.

The police officers who had done the arresting the previous night were usually on hand just in case someone locked up happened to plead not guilty.

Of the cast of lawyers who worked the court, Frank Sigsworth was unquestionably a certified genius, a great speaker, an expert in litigation, law, English, math, and science, and a performer in court. He often crossed verbal swords with Crown Prosecutor Alan Scales, which was always enjoyable. Allison Gillis, who successfully sued the city for closing Johnny Reid's business Johnny's Fish and Chips, was on the go. Another lawyer, who was one of the most knowledgeable and capable men in court, was Black Jack Nicholson. His cross examinations and "in your face" attitude had many police officers shaking in their boots.

Of course, there was the legendary Lester O'Donnell whose famous phrase "plead guilty, I'll get you off," still brings a chuckle. Lester convinced hundreds of his clients to plead guilty, which they could have done themselves and saved themselves the legal fees had they known the law. Unfortunately, few people did in those days. Some of Lester's clients paid in cash, some in cigarettes, and some in property. Often, Lester's fee was "a pint and $10.00," and if the client couldn't pay, he'd ask them for their watch as a down payment. They all paid eventually. The other side was that pleading guilty with Lester somehow reduced the penalty, which was an advantage. Pleading guilty saved the court time as witnesses and arresting police officers were not needed to testify, which often resulted in a less harsh or more favourable outcome for the guilty party.

If someone was unfortunate enough to have been arrested on Friday night, the task of getting off without a blemish had little to do with justice. Mostly, it depended on the strength of one's relationship with Bert Campbell, the Clerk of the Court. He would read the charges against the first man in row one to the Judge who presided over the proceedings. Campbell usually made comments to the Judge quietly but out of range of the accused. The accused or his lawyer would then plead guilty or not guilty. The not-guilty plea meant dragging out the proceedings. This aggravated the Judge who looked down from his elevated perch at the court, very much annoyed that court procedures had interrupted his reading of *The Guardian*, which by then was folded neatly in sections.

The Judge looked down on the proceedings much like the priest or minister when addressing his flock. A guilty plea pleased the court; however, before passing judgment, the Judge listened closely to the advice of the clerk who would add such comments as, "He's no good, Your Honour. None of his family is any good. May I suggest $25 dollars or 10 days?" and the show continued. In my two years covering the Police Court, I cannot recall Bert ever advocating for an individual who had been arrested on a Friday night. He wielded enormous influence in the court proceedings, so much so that he eventually joined the Bar. Bert was one of the last individuals to article with a law firm for legal training rather than graduate from a law school.

A Saturday morning court session, especially on a warm, sunny, summer day, was usually a marathon rather than a sprint. With a full docket of six or seven rows of clients, a not guilty plea could cause much grief. As mentioned, it interrupted the Judge, Albert James Haslam from reading his paper, and it also brought the Crown Prosecutor, Alan Scales into the play. He looked legal. He was tall and regal with a domineering air. He proved to be ruthless as a Crown Prosecutor, a modern-day

Captain Bly straight from the pages of R. L. Stevenson's novel *Mutiny on the Bounty*, without a hint of compassion.

Some suggested that on his nasty days, a hangover might have been the cause. Others suggested he was just born that way. I looked at it this way: if someone got past Bert Campbell's verbal abuse/advice to the Judge, it would be difficult to withstand the fury of the Crown Prosecutor. I concluded that the wily Lester O'Donnell probably offered the best advice: "Plead guilty and I'll get you off."

Alan Scales and Ray Murphy

In Scottish courts, there was a verdict that fell between guilty and not guilty, which was "not proven." It was a category that could have come in handy in those days.

One Saturday morning in July, the docket of prisoners awaiting their day in court was enormous, with all rows filled. It was 10:00AM, and after two not guilty pleas, the court was way behind schedule. The likelihood of finishing by noon was doubtful. The Court liked to wrap things up by noon in time for family matters, golf, or as a favour to *The Evening Patriot* and its 1:00PM deadline. A string of guilty pleas got the schedule back on track with Campbell offering his usual advice: "This man is no good and he's been before this court previously. Obviously hasn't learned his lesson. His brother has been here too. No good, Your Honour." By this time, Judge Haslam had neatly folded his newspaper and was halfway through *The Guardian* before checking his watch. A guilty plea, drunk and disorderly in a public place, twenty dollars or five days, next.

This continued for twenty minutes or so when a chap was charged with impaired driving. His lawyer, Sigsworth, pronounced, "Not guilty." It was a hot Saturday morning and, with a full docket, this declaration caused much turmoil as the *The Patriot* presses halted at 1:00PM, and the paper had to be out shortly thereafter.

The not guilty plea unleashed pandemonium in the courtroom. Sigsworth knew that the two arresting officers were notorious for not keeping accurate notes. He called the officers to the stand. Sigsworth started with "Your Honour [Haslam], my Learned Friend [Scales] the Crown Prosecutor," and gesturing to the seven rows, "invited guests," to which there was a thunderous burst of laughter. Of course, Judge Haslam urged

Sigsworth to move forward: "We have a large docket and it's extremely hot, so stop the theatrics."

Sigsworth began with an unusual line of questions: "What is your name, officer, your official name, not your nickname?" "You know me, Frank, it's Apps." This went on for five minutes until Sigsworth was sure the officer had forgotten about the previous night. Since the officers had already given evidence which direction the car had travelled, and the officer admitted that he was headed south, Sigsworth suggested that the court drop the case. He closed with, "I wonder who should have been charged, the officers or my client?"

Then there's the story about Keith MacLean and his passenger Roy Scantlebury, two of my friends who, after a night on the town, were flying down Kent Street and lost control of the car while making the turn on Kent and Great George. They plowed through the front door of the Charlottetown Liquor Store on Great George, which was right across from the present-day location of the Sportsmen Club. The story of a car going through the front door of the liquor store was a hot story for Charlottetown, and J. Pius was anxious to have this story on the front page. That Saturday morning, I noticed the duo sitting in the back row on the docket. I knew they would be hounding me to keep the story and their names out of Saturday's *Patriot*.

At the end of court, Roy, Keith, their lawyer Frank Sigsworth, and I went around the corner to the Town and and Country Restaurant for a tea and to plan how to exclude their names from the newspaper. Nevertheless, editor J. Pius was a tough newsperson, nothing escaped his attention, and in such matters, spared no one; he also was balanced and fair. I told all three that the best course of action was to stay at the Town and Country just beyond 1:00PM in the hope that *The Patriot* would print without the court news. They left just before 1:00PM with the understanding that we had missed the deadline. Shortly after they left, Pius phoned me at the Town and Country. He was furious, and told me to get the hell up to *The Guardian* office right away as he was holding the presses. *Patriot* photographer Sam Craswell had a great picture of the car in the liquor store.

I had no time to alert Roy and Keith, who had made plans to meet me at the Fire Hall at the back of the CFCY building next to the Charlottetown Hotel. After the blast from Pius, I put the cutline together and added more City Court information to be included on page three. The first editions of *The Patriot* showed the picture of the car and the names of Roy and Keith enlarged on the front page. I picked two or three papers hot off the press and headed to the Fire Hall to inform Roy and Keith.

Before I could open my mouth, the two thrust a beer into my hand and thanked me for what I had done. Roy quickly looked on page three to see if his name had appeared. For a few minutes, both were elated. Then Roy White, a Fire Hall regular, walked through the doors and congratulated both Roy and Keith on making the front page. Both men have since passed away. However, when they were still alive, they liked to remind me of this story when we used to get together for a pop or two.

● ● ●

My police court experiences introduced me to many of the local police officers: Police Chief Sterns Webster, Charlie Ready, Keith Wakelin, Duck Trainer, Shorty Williams, Red Taylor, Wayne Flynn, and many others. Keith Wakelin was usually on a motorcycle, wore high black leather boots, and, as my father said the first time he saw him, "he reminds me of a Gestapo Officer." Many Charlottetown citizens insist that Wakelin was the finest police officer ever to wear the police uniform. I agree.

After my court reporting days, it was not the end of my experiences with Alan Scales. A few years later, my mother started working at the Land Registry office to help support the growing family. One winter morning, a city truck slammed into her car and the driver insisted it was as much my mom's fault as it was his. Her car was heavily damaged and the city didn't intend to do anything about it.

I told Mom that the guy who was going with Patsy Shaw next door was Alan Scales. I told her that that guy was ruthless unless he was on the defense's side. A few days later, Mom collared Alan in front of 87 Upper Prince. He assured her that he would investigate her situation.

She went to his office, gave him the information he needed, and he told her she would be getting some news before the end of the month. Within a month, the city forwarded a cheque to Mom for damages and then some, much more than she had expected. It was enough for a new car. The court experience was more beneficial than expected—for my mom, anyway.

Years later, my friend Ray Murphy had a problem where a client/customer had attempted to sue Murphy Pharmacies for allegedly giving out the wrong medication. Technically, it was the wrong drug; in reality, they were identical just in different brand names. This was a big case for Ray, who was just starting out in his business, an issue of concern. Ray went to Alan Scales and asked him to take the case. Once the other legal team found out that Scales was representing Ray, they abandoned the case and it was dropped immediately.

Unfortunately, no City Police Court proceeding records were kept because they would make for interesting reading.

CHAPTER 6

Linotypes, Headlines and Harness Racing

THE EVENING PATRIOT, FIRST PUBLISHED ON JULY 1, 1864, has played a major role in the life cycle of Charlottetown. Its role was less in other parts of the Island at the latter part of the 20th century. Primarily a Liberal party newspaper, during the 1860s and 1870s, it came out strongly against Confederation and the building of the railway. Although PEI takes pride in being the birthplace of Confederation, the Island government—both Liberals and Conservatives—voted against Confederation and did not join the union until 1873.

For the first 50 years, the bias towards the Liberals continued but that started to subside by the beginning of the First World War. By the 1920s, *The Patriot* introduced a sports section, a comic section, and a women's page, all firsts for the Island print business. The editorials of the day discussed education, taxation, government spending, all from a Liberal perspective. In addition, the use of photographs was evident and proved to be extremely popular.

By the 1940s, political editorials gradually disappeared as Second World War news outweighed mentions of local happenings and developments. By the 1950s, the political editorials still looked at news from a Liberal viewpoint, however, a sense of balance was surfacing.

In 1957, Thomson Newspapers purchased the Patriot Publishing Company following a fire that destroyed *The Patriot* plant. From the 1960s onwards, *The Patriot* editorials avoided controversy to avoid offending its main source of revenue, its advertisers, or its readers from both sides of the political spectrum. It focused on a local coverage, strong sports section, and international news from outside sources like Canadian Press and Reuters.

Generally, *The Patriot* was viewed as Charlottetown's afternoon paper and, for a long time, it provided a terrific service. In the sports world, for example, night baseball and late-night games in all major sports provided partial scores in *The Guardian*, which "covers the Island like the dew," because it had a publishing deadline of 11:00PM Eastern. The pro games would not be completed by *The Guardian's* deadline, but full scores and stories were readily available in *The Patriot*.

The printing of a newspaper was laborious: *The Guardian* and *The Patriot* both carried a large group of typesetters, because every inch of the newspaper was cast in hot lead. The paper was arranged in reverse order so that when ink was applied and newsprint rolled over it, the paper printed. This method of printing was not only time-consuming but also labour-intensive, requiring proofreaders to ensure that there were no glaring errors. Additionally, the typesetters and all individuals working in the printing of the paper were unionized, which meant that there were no over-deadline stories.

Because of the noise, the linotype machines were located in the back section of the second floor of the main *Evening Patriot* office on Prince Street. The linotype machine is a line-casting machine used in printing, along with the letterpress printing, which was the industry standard for newspapers from the late

1800s until the early 1970s. The name of the machine comes from the fact that it produces an entire line of metal type at once, and was a great improvement over the letter-by-letter hand type-setting. The days of the hot metal typesetting, slugs, and the jobs of colourful *Patriot* typesetters such as Meryl Longaphie, Paul Taylor, and Gene Ward were ending, all victims of technology and cost-cutting. Lithography printing and computer typesetting were the new buzz words in the printing world.

Before the 1970s had run its course, the linotype jobs had disappeared and the new technology of cut and paste required fewer employees to put the paper together. The changes from 1967 to 1977 were dramatic. Where the second floor on Prince Street once housed 40-50 people such as reporters, page editors, photographers and their dark room, typesetters, and layout people, the number was less than half.

The Patriot also carried a large staff of reporters, writers, and at least two photographers, including Bill Taylor and Sam Craswell. J. Pius Callaghan, Dr. Harry Callaghan's father, was the editor of *The Patriot* who treated both Liberals and Conservatives fairly and firmly.

J. Pius was primarily a sports fan; therefore, hockey, base-ball, basketball, and harness racing had extensive coverage. The Callaghan Cup, which was presented annually to the Maritime Junior Hockey championship team, was named in memory of his role in the development of hockey in this region. With his heavy involvement in harness racing, he ensured that the cov-erage of harness racing at the Charlottetown Driving Park was second to none in North America. For many years, *The Evening Patriot* was the major sponsor of the Gold Cup and Saucer Race, one of the great races in the world of harness racing.

J. Pius also managed the pari-mutuels for the evening CDP race card, calculating the odds by pencil and paper, tallying the number of win tickets sold on each horse and the pool. The odds were forwarded via phone every minute to Lorne Yeo, who grew up on Park Street next door to the race track, running the tote board in the centre field. Jim McTague, Stu MacLure, Roger MacDonald, Don Chandler, and I worked as sellers or did the odds—with J. Pius supervising.

The *Evening Patriot* carried a harness racing story every race day, and printed a handicapping section, for example, the Railbird selections for regular fans and tourists. CDP co-owners Duck Acorn, Mel Jenkins, and Doug Hill were often at *The Patriot* office visiting with publisher Bill Hancox and J. Pius on harness racing activities. This group of five came up with the Gold Cup and Saucer concept. The afternoon paper had plenty of support with solid newspaper people, a committed and loyal following, and plenty of advertisers.

Lorne, who rose to the heights of news editor of *The Guardian-Evening Patriot,* started as a reporter covering the provincial and city court beats in 1965. He was there when I arrived during the summer break in 1967, and I was at his retirement gathering in 2003. Lorne's introduction to the newspaper business was similar to those looking for jobs in that era: more by luck or who was a friend than by great planning. *The Evening Patriot* photographer Bill Taylor urged Lorne to apply to work as a reporter. Since Lorne had a solid English grammar and writing background from teachers Father Frank Ledwell and Wendell "Pono" MacIntyre at St. Dunstan's, he did just that. He landed an interview with publisher W J William Hancox who asked Lorne only two questions: "Will you start for $30 a week and can you begin at 8:30AM on Monday?" He barked one condition, "Don't be late."

Lorne's early years growing up in Charlottetown were typical of many other young people those days. Money was always scarce. Because he grew up next door to the race track, he experienced horse racing and the smells and sounds of the midway that came with the Exhibition every August. Like me, he had an early connection to newspapers with a paper route. He also sold bottles, and smelts and night crawlers to anglers, anything to put a few dollars in his pocket. He raised $72 one summer on these assorted jobs and with it, bought a new double-bar CCM bike with large tires from Art Burns at the Bike Shop. His first summer job was working at Maurice Block's junk yard on Kent Street, where DVA is now, loading beer bottles and scrap metal onto trucks. His mother Norma's shop, "Norma's Ladies Wear," was in the Block building. No doubt Norma had something to do with her son's summer employment.

As interesting as Lorne's early days were, his family background was more fascinating. His grandfather was Harry Thom, who had emigrated from Canton, China, and married Rachel Samson, a Newfoundland girl. Harry operated the Roxy Restaurant, one of three Chinese restaurants operating in the city in the 1940s and 1950s. It was located on Great George St. opposite today's Dow's Menswear. Another Chinese establishment was the New England Café, today the Canton Restaurant, operated by Harry's brother Ben Thom. George Lee later operated the Canton for many years. The other Chinese restaurant, the Island Grill, opposite Corney's Shoe Store on Queen Street, was run by Walter Lee.

The Yeos, including mother Norma and father Ralph, Lorne and his siblings Harry and Leah moved to Villa Avenue in 1960.

Sadly, their mother Norma died from brain cancer at 39, leaving a gaping hole in the family. A little more than four years after her passing, Lorne started his career in the news paper business with *The Evening Patriot* and it was love at first sight.

Lorne's first day was January 5, 1965; he and veteran city beat reporter Ralph Cameron covered city council. Cameron, who wrote the popular column "Coffee Cup" for many years, gave him his first piece of advice: "Start writing now and don't stop till it's over. Listen closely and get it written down right, so the coverage is accurate."

The 1960s were the heyday of newspapers and there were numerous dedicated newspaper veterans such as Neil "Tiny" Matheson, a giant and a former football player, who wrote "Across the Island" from regularly-recorded interviews. J. Pius was the managing editor. Ralph Cameron produced editorials when needed quickly. Stan Bowles edited special editions and features. Burton Lewis was an editorial writer. Frank Walker was chief editor. Frank was knowledgeable in all aspects of newspaper coverage and was a highly-regarded legislative writer. He recorded the proceedings in the PEI Legislature before *Hansard* evolved. Frank was the last word on anything a reporter needed to know about the mechanics of writing. Lorne also had the benefit to working with Don MacLeod and Bill Burnett, excellent editors who have long since passed away.

Lorne passed on two stories to me: the first had to do with his coverage of City Police Court activity and a headline that appeared in page three of *The Evening Patriot*. The headline read, "Ralph Herbert Yeo, well-known Charlottetown businessman, pleaded guilty of drunk driving." As expected, that headline generated so much turmoil at home that his father banned Lorne from the household. Lorne went to live with Aunt Mona for the next three weeks until his dad called and allowed him to come home. From that moment, nobody questioned whether a name was left out of City Police Court. Everyone respected Lorne's objectivity.

The other story involved Alex Campbell, then-premier, who called *The Patriot* office livid about a story that Lorne had written concerning the pending strike of C.N. Rail. In the article, Lorne noted that Alex Campbell, "was not available for comment." He was furious about some of the material, especially the "not available" comment. However, Lorne had "inside sources" and he was not about to reveal them. Campbell told Lorne that he was informing his staff that Lorne Yeo was not permitted inside the premier's suite from that day forward. Since it was part of Lorne's job to interview MLAs and/or the Premier, this action placed the reporter in a difficult situation.

That same evening around 7:30PM, the phone rang in the Yeo household and Lorne answered. "This is Alex Campbell speaking, and I thought I would call and clarify our misunderstanding today. I am on my way home but you can meet me in my office tomorrow at 8:30AM." The next morning, the Premier was still annoyed and asked Lorne for his confidential news source. He refused.

The Premier butted his cigarette and surprised Lorne when he said, "Ok, what questions do you have for me today?" That interview produced four, front page stories.

To this day, Lorne insists that Alex Campbell was PEI's greatest premier because of his honesty and respect for people. And, I've always maintained that Lorne Yeo, former assistant managing editor of The Evening Patriot and later the night editor of The Guardian, was happiest with a newspaper or a manuscript in his hands. This holds true from day one in 1965 until now.

When *The Evening Patriot* folded on June 9, 1995, Lorne was assigned as the main editor of *The Guardian*, where he stayed until his retirement in 2003. Gary MacDougall was named managing editor until he retired in 2016 after nearly 50 years in the local newspaper business. *The Guardian* was sold to the SaltWire Network out of Halifax in April 2017. Shortly after that, Dave MacKenzie was named publisher and Wayne Thibodeau was regional editor.

For 18 months from 1963-65, I attended St. Dunstan's while working off-and-on at the newspaper. I had a chance meeting at Prince of Wales College (PWC) with Lorne Moase, who later became the Deputy Minister of Education, which changed my education status. At that time, education in the province was desperately short of male teachers, so Mr. Moase provided me with a $500 grant each semester and I was enrolled in Miss Yeo's Education class at PWC. I enrolled and successfully completed the courses over two years, but lost every dollar betting on the horses at the Charlottetown Driving Park and Sackville Downs in Halifax. To get by, I borrowed the books I needed for school from George Bendelier, a fellow gambler who worked for businessman Hugh Simpson and owned a book store.

I was more interested in the money for betting than teaching, but the schooling helped later, as my father had said it would.

As much as I enjoyed the newspaper business, during the summer and winter of 1967-68, the urge to move on and out of Charlottetown was too strong. When George "Lefty" Dunn, one of the best left-handed pitchers to come out of PEI, called me in May of 1968 with an offer to play senior baseball in Orillia, Ontario, I didn't hesitate. Armed with a few dollars from Mom and the advice my father gave me about leaving the newspaper business—"nothing one learned is ever truly useless"—I headed to Ontario on the train.

CHAPTER 7

Orillia or Buist Championship or Bust

A JOB, A COTTAGE WITH ANOTHER IMPORTED PLAYER, and money on the side may not sound like much today, but it was a pretty good deal in early 1968. I had never heard of Orillia and had no idea where it was, but I was young, so everything looks great. Baseball was my first love and since the game on PEI had dropped in popularity compared to fastball, it made my decision that much easier. The fastball teams in Charlottetown were better organized and had money behind them. Soon the best players in the province, guys like Tex, Bobby Rice, and Emmett Ellsworth, moved from baseball at Memorial Field to the City Diamond just across the street.

I was some excited to be away for the first time on my own, and I was glad to get out of Charlottetown. I needed a change of scenery. I went by bus with my Legion teammate Wayne MacDougall and junior pitcher Jon Down from Charlottetown to the train station in Amherst. Once on the train, I went immediately to the bar car, and then via rail to Orillia.

Orillia, I found out, was near Barrie, just north of Toronto. Orillia was like Charlottetown in that it was basically a tourist town, packed in the summer and back to a more relaxed atmosphere in the winter. Orillia also operated one of the very first hockey schools in the summer months as the Bobby Orr-Mike Walton hockey school had begun that same summer outside Orillia.

I sure was glad to see Lefty Dunn waiting for me in Orillia. He had just come up from Toronto where he lived and was in time for practice sessions in early May. My roommates turned out to be Bobby Smyth from Toronto, a crafty right-handed pitcher, and Chris Harbour from Ottawa, a good left-handed pitcher. Smyth or "Nifty" was a great guy and had known Johnny "Hawk" Martin from Charlottetown who grew up about 200 yards from our place on Spring Street. It was hard to understand where these two had met because the Smyth family in Toronto employed maids at their house in the west end of Toronto, and I am certain there were no maids ever employed in the Spring Park Road, Chestnut Street, Spring Street and Churchill Avenue area where the Martins grew up in Charlottetown. Nifty took me on my first visit to Toronto and to his home located not far from the The Old Mill subway stop.[5]

As Nifty would say, the 1968 Orillia team was just ordinary; we had a few top players but not enough to challenge any of the top senior clubs of this era. Before returning to PEI in the fall of 1968, I told General Manager Keith Speerin to get better players or I would not be back as I'd be better off playing with the PEI baseball team in the 1969 Canada Games in Halifax. It was a wait-and-see game.

• • •

When I returned to Orillia in the spring of 1969, a big, good-looking personable catcher named Wally MacMillan was waiting for me at the train station. He had played pro the previous summer with Phoenix in the San Francisco Giants organization and he certainly looked the part. In practice later that week, he showed a terrific arm—a cannon—was an excellent receiver, and a big swinger with power. He was easily the best catcher that I had ever played with.

He lived in a place called Little Britain with his wife Mary where they were raising a young family. However, hanging out with a single guy like me and with another single guy—Mike Buist—whom I was about to meet, didn't help Wally's married life.

We played in the Simcoe County League with teams like Alliston, Midland—that had ex-pro pitcher Gord Dyment— and Beeton that had Johnny and Larry Gould, Wayne Carleton, and Jimmy Rutherford. We also played in the Eastern Ontario League with Kingston, Belleville, Toronto East, and in as many tournaments as possible, even in Cooperstown, New York

It didn't take long to realize that Buist was not just an ordinary pitcher; in fact, an exhibition game at Christie Pitts in Toronto against the Toronto Maple Leafs' Senior baseball club made players on both teams take notice. Speerin promised

Mike Buist in his days with the New York Mets organization. He was the ace of the 1969 OBA Senior champions Orillia Majors.

In Loving Memory Of

Michael Buist
1947 - 2019

that he would sign a big starter, a guy from Hamilton, who had already pitched pro for three or four years in the New York Mets' and St Louis Cardinals' organizations. Speerin showed me a copy of *Baseball Digest*, which had ranked Buist among the top major league prospects.

Another newcomer that first exhibition game in Toronto was Chuck Beaudoin from Hamilton. He had been at a Pittsburgh Pirates camp and looked very good. He was a good hitting outfielder who ended up hitting second in our lineup. Another Hamilton boy, Nick Owen, who was Buist's close friend, was the best first baseman and leading hitter in the Inter-County League, and he decided to move to Orillia as well. Our team was starting to look like a championship contender. I was very pleased, playing centre and left field, and occasionally third and shortstop. Our infield also looked great with Owen at first, speedster and hard-hitting Pat Hennessey at second, veteran and sure-handed Curly Cockburn at short-stop, while third base was split between veteran Tex Howard and young Jerry Udell.

Wanting to keep Wally MacMillan in Orillia full-time, Otaco Steele GM Speerin secured permanent employment for him, and part-time work for Buist and me working occasionally as quality control officers. The work was just enough to maintain our weekly poker games with some people in the Orillia Greek community, and a few trips to Greenwood Raceway in Toronto when we had days off.

To raise money for the team, Speerin arranged for me to fight an exhibition boxing match against Orillia's Walter Henry with Buist acting as boxing promoter and trainer. He and I were to get $500 each and the team would clear about $3000 for the exhibition fight. Buist convinced me that with the boxing experience I had at home, I could easily beat Henry. Speerin's training schedule consisted of beer after every game, four or five games a week, Chinese food every second day, lots of spaghetti, poker every evening even after road games, and rest until noon if work didn't get in the way.

As the fight neared, interest swelled in the town and Leafs' defenceman Ricky Ley bet that hometown boy Walter Henry would clean my clock. Ricky's brother Ron always chirped to me at the ball games insisting he'd love to see Walter knock my block off, which I insisted couldn't possibly happen. I hadn't heard of the 5' 5" Walter before. However, since we always had eight-ounce boxing gloves at home and I knew how to fight, I figured I would win easily. Buist and I began to have doubts when we started to notice the pictures in the Orillia store windows of Walter winning amateur titles all around the world against top ranked fighters. Walter also worked at Otaco Steel, and he and I had the chance to speak often as the exhibition boxing match neared. Then Walter was injured and the fight didn't take place. Buist and I got our money up front, but it was all gone, thanks to cards and horses. Such an anti-climax.

• • •

The Orillia Majors played in numerous tournaments across Ontario, numerous times at Christie Pits against Toronto Maple Leafs and Leaside Maple Leafs, in Cooperstown, New York, where we were billed as Ontario All-Stars vs Cooperstown Macks, a team of mostly ex-pros from that area of New York State. One of the guys with us in Cooperstown was outfielder Barry Smith from Oshawa who played with Team Canada in 1972 in Moncton when Vern Handrahan was pitching coach. Orillia's goal was to represent Ontario at the 1969 Summer

Games in Halifax, or failing that, to win the Ontario Senior Crown against London or Stratford, the top inter-county clubs.

In the tournament to decide the Ontario winner and the trip to Halifax, we won three straight games but lost to the Inter-County All-stars 2-0 in a pitching duel between Buist and Ron Stead of Guelph. I had not faced Stead before but he didn't throw a strike near the middle of the plate; he was that crafty. We had three straight left-handed hitters at the top of our line-up: Chuck Beaudoin, Pat Hennessey (very good, switch-hitter), and myself at 1-2-3. Right-handed slugger Nick Owen was the leading hitter in the Inter-County League the previous year in the four slot, with MacMillan fifth and Ken Hipwell sixth in the line-up.

The Inter-County team that beat us in this tournament captured the Gold medal in Halifax with ease as they had more quality pitching than the other provinces. Besides Stead, who had pitched for the first ever Team Canada Baseball team in 1967 and is regarded as the greatest pitcher ever to play in the Inter-County Baseball League, the Inter-County club also had top right-handers Rick Birmingham and Brian Murphy, among others. Had we won, we would have had Buist, Gord Dyment, and Lefty Dunn as well as Stead, Birmingham, and Murphy. I'm sure we could also have beaten any of the teams in Halifax, but not going to Nova Scotia to play against the guys from the Island with whom I had grown up and won championships, hurt a little.

Since we didn't win the right to go to the Canada Games, our number two goal was the Ontario Senior championship against the best teams in Ontario. We knew were as good as, if not better than, the other top teams. Our chances got better with the addition of Midland's Gord Dyment to join Buist and Lefty Dunn. We got stronger down the playoff trail and made it to the final against London Pontiacs, the top club in the Inter-County League. London had barely made it past the Stratford Hoods, which had several USA college players including eventual San Francisco all-star short-stop Chris Speier.

The best of five series opened in London and they won the first game. We won the next game in Orillia, then they won at home in London. We won at home in Orillia, setting the stage for the OBA Senior crown at London. The London Pontiacs flew in their big left-handed ace Carl Moharter from California, but Mike Buist simply dominated giving up just two unearned runs and only four hits; he was extra fast and more than lived up to advance billings. He was the best pitcher I ever played with, although I also played for years with PEI's Mike Kelly; he was extra special, too.

The win was the 21st of the season for Buist who pitched over 220 innings that summer, a tough act in amateur baseball. In the championship game win, I scored the tying run and drove in the winning run as we took a 4-2 lead before close friend Wally MacMillan blasted a home run into dead centre to make it a 5-2 Orillia victory. Moharter, who had lost just once against eleven wins, gave up nine hits while Buist was skilled giving up four singles. In my opinion, Buist was the best pitcher in Canada at that time.

In that series, we had beaten all three of their ace pitchers—Moharter, Birmingham, and Murphy—in winning the best of five series. They had a terrific club as well with shortstop Brian Pearen, Paul Allen, Arden Eddie, and Whitey Lapthorne, as well as Ty Crawford from Toronto who played in the US college

ranks. The Inter-County had numerous American imports at
the time: guys like Chris Speier from San Francisco who, three
years later, played in the major league all-star game with the
San Francisco Giants, and Bill Lee's brother who played in
Brampton. Moharter later pitched with the LA Dodgers. All the
teams in the Inter County were strong and some of the guys
that I remember included the middle infield combination of Alf
Payne and Robbie Stevens from Toronto, who were outstanding.

During the summer of 1969, there was a break in the baseball schedule, and, while having breakfast downtown in Orillia
one morning, I noticed a headline in the *Toronto Star:*

"A Genuine Tip from Shakey Louie," penned by Milt
Dunnell. It was a story on the 1969 Maple Leaf Trot. Being
harness racing fans, my roommate Buist and I borrowed GM
Keith Speerin's blue thunderbird and headed to Greenwood
Raceway for the Trot on Saturday night. Buist enjoyed the races
so it was an easy trip to Toronto, although I was sure glad he did
the driving; the four-lane traffic was not for me.

We arrived at Greenwood about an hour before the races
and searched out where the former Islanders were. That
included Johnny "Hawk" Martin and Lloyd "Say" Doiron, who
informed me that the Director of Security for the Ontario
Jockey Club was none other than our former City Baseball
League umpire Bill Coughlan who had travelled with Forbie
Kennedy and Charlie Ryan when stationed in Charlottetown.
Martin told me that the guy we all knew as Kenny Ford was the
caretaker of Maple Leaf Trot contender Grandpa Jim, for owner
of the Lloyd Arnold Cattle Company, with Robert Farrington
driving. In addition, Joe O'Brien would be driving Fresh
Yankee in the big race. Kenny Ford and another guy, both from

Charlottetown, were working as grooms/caretakers. They had come a long way since the days of driving milk wagon horses in Charlottetown.

Bill Coughlan was glad to see me and more than willing to give us a couple of paddock passes so we'd have a chance to see Ford. Of course, it was a busy evening with security officials near Grampa Jim. When I introduced Ford to Buist, I blurted "This is Kenny Ford." He motioned to me to be quiet, "I'm now Lou Forbes, aka 'Shaky Louie'. That's what I go by in the USA." We had a brief chat and he told Buist and me that his horse was sharp right now with a big chance to win.

Grandpa Jim won easily. It was one of those rare occasions that a tip came through. Three decades later in 2005 at the Little Brown Jug in Delaware, Ohio, top USA trainer Erv Miller introduced me to his owner Lloyd Arnold. I told him that I met him years earlier at Greenwood Raceway, the night his trotter Grandpa Jim won the Maple Leaf Trot. We both had a great chuckle.

● ● ●

The year 1969 was memorable for the MacDonald brothers: I won the Ontario Senior A crown, and on the Island, Tex and Jack Middleton's Towers Mud Hens won the Maritime Intermediate A Crown with teammates Bobby Rice, Emmett Ellsworth, Roy MacGonnell, Roger Gallant, and ace righty John MacKinnon. The year was also one that hockey fans on PEI will remember.

CHAPTER 8

The Charlottetown Hockey Islanders

SHORTLY AFTER THE BASEBALL SEASON ENDED IN mid-October in Orillia, the hockey season opened with an exhibition game between the Allan Cup-bound Orillia Terriers and Buffalo, the New York Rangers farm club. One Friday evening, I received a call from my buddy, Wally MacMillan, to tell me that Forbes Kennedy, long-time friend and the only PEI player in the NHL at the time, was on the Buffalo roster and expected to play. Forbie, who set an NHL record for penalty minutes in a playoff game with the Toronto Maple Leafs against the Bruins in April 1969, had undergone a knee operation in the summer. He'd been picked up by Emile Francis, then-GM of the New York Rangers. Fred Shero, who had won championships everywhere in the Rangers organization, coached Buffalo, and he had a veteran team including goaltender Gilles Villemure, Wayne Rivers, Forbie, and defenceman Sheldon Kannegiesser.

I watched in disbelief as Forbie hobbled around the ice during the game. After the game, he could barely walk let alone skate. I knew that Forbie would never be back in the National Hockey League again. His knee operation had been a disaster. Once back on the Island, the only hockey Forbie played was the occasional exhibition game when ex-NHLers would come to town for charity fund-raising events.

At that time of the season, the Orillia team was adding players for their Allan Cup run and GM Bill McGill asked about players from the Maritimes. Two names he had heard were Oscar Gaudet and Phil Doiron of Moncton. I told them that neither one would leave Moncton but that Paul MacWilliams, a right-handed shooting defenceman or forward from Summerside was a great shot, and was a possibility. They checked his stats with the Halifax Junior Canadians, and as an All-Canadian with St. Dunstan's University, and were interested. I contacted MacWilliams in Summerside and twice the Orillia people arrived at the Toronto airport but Paul did not show. I talked to Paul's dad Bruce who told me that Paul decided to go to Buchans with Lloyd "Toy Toy" Gallant. As it turned out, it was the mistake of a lifetime. The Terriers then added another right-handed shooting defenceman named Claire Alexander, who was a big star as Orillia won the Allan Cup. The Orillia goaltender was Gerry McNamara, who, a few years later, became the GM of the Toronto Maple Leafs bringing Orillia defence-man Alexander with him.

I headed back to PEI in April 1970 in time to watch the famous PEI Junior Islanders sideline the Ottawa M&M Rangers, and future all-star Larry Robinson, in the Eastern Canada Memorial Cup quarter-finals. The Islanders had a powerful club with future NHLers like Bob MacMillan, Al McAdam, and Hill Graves, and a great supporting cast with guys like Alex Dampier, Tommy and Timmy Steeves, Angus Beck, Dave Murnaghan, Peter Williams, and goaltender Ray Gibbs. Head Coach Jack Hynes and General Manager Norman "Hawk" Larter formed an unlikely duo: the soft spoken, quiet Hynes and the fiery rhetoric of "The Hawk," who preached Memorial Cup from his first breath in the morning.

In the semi-finals, the Islanders were up against the Quebec Remparts, a club that included Jacques Richard, André Savard, Michel Brier, goalie Gilles Meloche, and Guy LaFleur. At that time, Lafleur was the talk of the junior hockey world setting scoring records first with the Aces, then the Remparts. At the Remparts' first practice in the historic Charlottetown Forum, 1,500 Islanders took in their practice, a sure indication of the hype about this big series. The Remparts were heavy favorites and the opening game at the Charlottetown Forum was sold out an hour after tickets went on sale. The Islanders opened on a Sunday afternoon with 2,700 fans, sounding more like 4,000, leaning over the boards and cussing the Remparts' players a few feet away, creating a frenzied atmosphere for visiting players. The Islanders stunned the Remparts, winning 3-1 in a rough-and-tough contest, setting the stage for an even more chaotic game two.

Game two was the next night, and the frenzy continued where it had left off. Fights broke out early and often, the first between Islanders' tough guy Gordie Gallant and Remparts' Réjean Giroux, continuing off-and-on until late in the third period. By that time, the Islanders had built up a 6-4 lead, and, as expected both benches emptied, and the game was called with four minutes left on the clock. Fights broke out in the stands and in the street outside the Forum. André Savard was arrested after the game, and let out in time to catch the bus to the Ferry, a bus that was pelted with eggs, potatoes, and anything else that could be hurled. The Island fans chased the bus to the ferry with police protection all the way.

The Remparts protested the game, the ending of the contest, and the alleged police brutality. Over the next 24 hours, the Attorney General of PEI, the Attorney General of Quebec, and J. Pius Callaghan, President of the Maritime Junior hockey League, met to iron-out the situation.

The Remparts protest was tossed out and the series shifted to Quebec City where the hospitality was just as friendly as in Charlottetown. The Remparts won the next three in Quebec; the last game's score was 10-1, which just about brought an end to the Islanders Memorial Cup dreams. When the series shifted back to the Island, the Islanders had nothing left, losing before another packed house 6-2.

Yet, what Island fans did not know was that the one player who may have greatly boosted the Islanders' chances of upsetting Quebec in this series was junior eligible Errol Thompson. Thompson had quit the Halifax Junior Canadians the previous spring and was playing senior hockey with the Charlottetown-based Sandys Royals. Islanders GM Hawk Larter had signed Thompson to a junior card for the 1969-70 series, but Errol had also signed a senior card with Sandy Frizzell, the sponsor of Sandys Royals. Had Hawk turned in the Islanders card with Thompson's signature, Errol would have been ineligible to play any hockey, junior or senior, thus the card disappeared.

It was PEI's finest hour in junior hockey and, for most hockey fans who follow the game on the Island, the greatest junior hockey team ever iced by a Charlottetown team of any era. Even today, almost 50 years later, Island hockey fans are haunted by the "what ifs" had Errol Thompson played with the Junior Islanders in that series.

At the end of the great run by the Charlottetown Hockey Islanders, I headed back to Ontario and joined Buist in Hamilton with the Inter-County Red Wings. The stay didn't last long. Unfortunately, shortly after arriving I broke my ankle at the Civic Stadium and that was the end of my baseball days. I headed back to PEI not knowing what to do and not ready to return to university.

Mike, a McMaster graduate, went on to become marketing manager in Canada for Labatt Brewing, and worked for many years with PEI's Don MacDougall who was President of Labatt and responsible for bringing the Blue Jays to Canada. In fact, Buist worked in various roles for the Toronto Blue Jays in those early years. As marketing manager of Labatt, Buist was responsible for numerous properties including the Labatt Tankard, or the Brier. Buist, who often travelled to the Island for meetings with curling folks like Gerry Muzika, president of the Charlottetown Curling Club. Gerry, who with my help, recruited Mike to spearhead a fundraiser at the City club to eliminate its mortgage, thereby ensuring continuous curling in the centre of Charlottetown. Buist also met numerous colourful characters including Gerry "Soupy" Campbell who pitched an idea to Buist:

"I will cover the world curling championships in Germany, and relay back daily reports to Canadian media via radio on the happenings at the world championships sponsored by Labatt Breweries. All you have to do is pay for the flights."

In mid-summer, long after the world championships in Germany had ended, and long-after Buist had thought that he had put the world curling championships' file to bed, letters to his attention starting arriving at Labatt's; bills for lodging and travel associated with Soupy's assignment arrived. Mike just shook his head and laughed. He liked Soupy.

Sadly, Mike passed away in St. John's, Newfoundland, in October 2019, where he was the director of baseball and a popular figure in the city.

CHAPTER 9

A Bachelor's Life of Horses, Gloves and Fastballs

I HADN'T BEEN TO ROYAL MILITARY COLLEGE IN
Kingston nor had I met my sister Bernadine's husband, Robin
Boadway, a low key individual. His original degree from Queens
is in Engineering. On his Rhodes Scholarship to Oxford, he
studied Economics, returning to Queens for his PhD, where
he has had a distinguished career. Robin is one of the world's
leading public economists and tax scholars. He has been asked
to speak on economic matters throughout the world, including
PEI, and has written several books on the topic. He is also an
Officer in the Order of Canada, among a long list of other
accomplishments. That's a tough act to follow.

Of course, Bernadine is no slouch: a top student all through
school, and president of the Charlottetown Nursing School
Student Council. She has always been my favourite—don't tell
the others—probably because we are closer in age. Likely—or
at least I like to think—it's because we take a more worldly look
at issues and with a more liberal dose of common sense. Among
such a distinguished group of people at their 1970 wedding at
RMC, for once I took my mother's advice and just listened.

Back in PEI, I contemplated going back to university but decided against it especially when my beer-drinking buddy Turk Osborne landed me a job at Canada Packers, at that time one of the best paying companies on the Island. Shaking hides was a tough, bloody job, but it gave me a hefty bank account and enough money to play the ponies, a little fastball, and drink beer.

Richard Bradley, another of my close friends, was working for James "Roach" MacGregor at the time. He encouraged me to think of harness racing, not as a trainer-driver but on the management side of the business, perhaps as a race secretary or in a race office. In those days, the Maritimes raced under the rules of the USTA and remained in that jurisdiction until 2000 when they joined Standardbred Canada. Bradley had worked for Stanley Dancer in the USA for decades and for Roach MacGregor in the Maritimes. The more I thought about his suggestion, the more I liked it.

I contacted the United States Trotting Director on PEI, Paul MacKinnon, and scheduled to write my Race Secretary USTA license during the winter of 1970-71.[6]

I had my papers in Spring 1971, just in time for the opening at the Fredericton Raceway, which needed a full-time GM and race secretary and which landed in my lap. My Charlottetown buddies Wally McInnis and Mike Campbell, who each operated a public stable, called and told me I could live with them as they had an apartment there.

I took the job at Wilmot Downs, which proved to be a great experience. Colin Campbell from Charlottetown worked at the Fredericton radio station, and soon he and I had a neat harness racing show that helped promote the track and encourage betting on the ponies. In addition, I got plenty of help and advice from former Islander Ingham Palmer who was the track announcer and promotions man at Saint John's Exhibition Park. Some veteran horsemen pitched in and helped make Fredericton a big success that summer.

Rufin Barrieau, a great horseman and one of the best all-around Maritime trainer-drivers, came up on race days every Tuesday and Thursday from Moncton with horses like Painter Blue, The Sketcher, and Miss Lulu S, while Laurie O'Brien, who usually raced at Sackville Downs in Halifax, stayed with us in Fredericton racing his horses, the top-class pacer Thinks Dream, and Esquire Boy. He and his wife Helen were people everybody loved.

Fred "Fiddler" MacDonald, General Manager and Race Secretary at Fredericton Raceway, extreme left, joins officials in the winners circle. Owner-driver Sheldon Campbell holds Snow Swift after his victory in the 1971 Fall Pacing championship at Wilmot Downs, aka Fredericton Raceway.

The Fredericton Exhibition in early September also attracted PEI-based horsemen, such as Francis McIsaac, Alex and Angus MacPhee, and Blois MacPhail. The horses they brought, top pacers like Mr. Jollity, Lexington, and Stephen Dale, helped bolster the race cards during the big week. Owner Gordon MacKinnon from PEI stayed the entire week with his driver Gerald Noonan and horses such as J. Scotch Hal, Indian Rock Chief, and Kim Sue.

Living with Wally McInnis and Mike Campbell in the basement apartment of Russell Embleton's house was quite an experience as Mike and Wally contributed little more than verbal support when it came time to getting the meals on the table. Their assistance sometimes included peeling a few potatoes, which should have been easy for any Islander.

That summer, Russell Embleton's Warbucks Pick raced against the best Invitational horses in the region; occasionally, we crossed into Maine for racing. Embleton's son Brian often travelled with us when travelling with Fredericton-based horses. Since neither Mike nor Wally ever drank, sometimes Brian could be coaxed into having a beer with me on the way back to Fredericton, frowned upon and against the law today, but back then a common occurrence.

The season in 1971 was enjoyable and profitable, setting a record bet on Walter Dale night, and sustaining a much-improved bet over the previous year, thanks in part to the support from Island horsemen and Rufin Barrieau from Moncton. It was a year that ensured I would be in the harness racing game in some capacity somewhere for a very long time.

I was laid off in early October and moved back to PEI. I realized this later, but that experience taught me that harness racing in the Maritimes was not a full-time job for administrators. Employment would always be seasonal. Teaching school with the summers off suddenly became very appealing. Plus, there is something to be said for job security and satisfaction.

When I returned to PEI, I decided to finish my Education degree and get on with my life. The fastball playoffs were in full swing and Tex had put together a powerful team anchored by our brothers, especially slick, second-sacker Rabs who would be the infield general for the MacDonald teams for the next 15 years. Rabs was a top student as evident by the fact that he was 15 in grade 12 at St. Dunstan's Senior High, but he never could get along with Father Cameron and a couple of the other priests. One day he walked out the door and didn't go back. He spent a few years in Fort McMurray before coming home for good.

I also got a chance that fall to watch the Junior Fastball Fawcetts in the City Fastball League playoffs, which featured a number of colourful and talented characters in shortstop Gary "Sput" MacDonald, infielders Paul Gormley and Mike Quinn, and slugging outfielders Mike Kennedy, Shane Dowling, and Stevie Gallant.

On the hockey front, the Charlottetown Junior Islanders were once again the big sports drawing card on the Island and, despite losing Bob MacMillan and Hillard Graves, they iced another strong Junior club that filled the old Charlottetown Forum every night they played.

The winter of 1971 brought about a story that is still talked about with laughter no matter how many times it is told. Boxing had been a sport that had a strong following on PEI in the 1940s, 1950s, and 1960s, with many pro boxing cards. By the 1970s, however, it had gone the way of the village blacksmith. We had always had boxing gloves at our house, and both Dad and Mom encouraged the boys to box to be sure we knew how to take care of ourselves. Uncle John Bradley had fought on a few cards at the old Sporting Club in Charlottetown, and we went to some pro cards at the Charlottetown Forum, which featured Gaston Roy, Tiger Steele, Don "Duck" Trainer, and others. At home on Spring Street, the boys would often try one another, and when the blood starting to flow, Mom put an end to the fights.

Gary/Sput wanted to go the Canada Games and the winter sports offered a possibility as amateur boxing was one of the sports on the Canada Games menu. He won the right to represent PEI at the 1971 Canada Games in Saskatoon by winning his championship fight at Confederation Centre, one of the few times a fight was held at the theatre. At the Games in Saskatoon, Sput won three straight fights and advanced to the semi-final. Of all people, he was against my old working buddy from Otaco Steel in Orillia, Walter Henry.

Henry had boxed for Canada in the 1964 and 1968 Olympics, and won a medal at the 1967 Pan Am Games. He was the Canadian featherweight champion nine times and, nearing the end of his illustrious boxing career, he had posted an almost unheard of 403 wins—18 losses. Henry asked Sput if he was any relation to Freddy MacDonald, and had a little chuckle when he heard Sput was one of my brothers.

As the story goes, before the second round, Walter hustled over to Sput's corner and touched gloves. Sput responded, "You don't touch gloves until the last round." Henry responded, "This is your last round." The fight was stopped, but Sput has not forgotten the day. After the fight, a reporter asked Sput what it was like fighting the veteran Henry. He replied, "He was very fast and skillful. I couldn't hit him with a hand full of rice."

That fight put an end to Sput's boxing career. In the ring, at least. He soon joined Tex and Rabs on the fastball diamond where he starred first as shortstop, and then catcher, by far the most talented catcher ever to come out of Prince Edward. He had a powerful and accurate throwing arm; he was a sure-handed receiver and a big hitter, later earning All Canadian honours at that position at the National Senior Men's Tournament.

Between 1969 and 1976, fastball flourished not just on PEI but throughout Atlantic Canada, and the Dartmouth Dairy Queen, under the guidance of Head Coach Howie Speers, dominated the game in Atlantic Canada. Speers was and still is

Dons Fawcetts, PEI Senior Champions
Back Row; left to right: Wayne MacDougall, Tom Gauthier, Smelt Gillis, Bobby Power, Joe Reardon, Brian McVicar, Mike Flanagan, Don MacLean, Gordie Power (MGR); Front Row: Harry Toombs, Joe Gallant, Sput MacDonald, Robin Hood, Ray Dunn, Todd Doyle (batboy), Joey Martin, Tex MacDonald, Sock MacDonald. (Missing for photo Sandy MacDonald).

regarded as one of the smartest baseball-fastball coaches in the Atlantic region.

In the 1950s and early 1960s on PEI, only the catcher and first baseman used a glove. By the mid-1960s with the rise of the "whip or windmill" pitching combined with power of opposing hitters, position players began using gloves. The speed of the game and the skill of the players attracted a new group of fans who found the entertainment and length of the games more desirable than baseball, like soccer's popularity today.

Speers was player and assistant coach with the Mahars' Transfer team that had won the Halifax league in 1966 and 1967, as well as the Maritime crown, in 1967. Mahars had top players like Speers who was league MVP, the great Lyle Carter who was the batting champion, first baseman Bob Forbes, and second baseman Doug Harvey. In 1969, Speers convinced Dartmouth Dairy Queen owner Peter Foy to sponsor his power-ful club in the hopes of a Maritime crown.

Dartmouth was not necessarily a lock for the 1969 Maritime Senior Men's title that year as softball had enjoyed enormous growth in New Brunswick: in the championship final, pitcher Stan Hennigar led the Moncton Viponds to the Maritime crown outdueling Halifax Keiths and pitcher Pete Devana in the best of three series. Phil Doiron had a couple of key hits in the Moncton victory.

In 1969, Speers was the player and assistant coach on the Nova Scotia, Canada Games team. His good friend and my brother Tex were standouts with the PEI team under the leadership of Willis Hennessey. In the Halifax Games' tournament, coach Hennessey went to his bullpen as Nova Scotia loaded the bases with one out and slugger Denny Clyke at the plate. The conversation on the mound went something like: "Can you get this guy out," barked Willis to relief pitcher Daryl "Diddles" Doyle. "Don't worry coach, I will get us out of this big hole, you can count on me," chirped Doyle. On the first pitch, Clyke hit it a country mile, which brought another trip to the mound by Hennessey. Before Willis opened his mouth, Diddles said, "I got us out of the hole."

Another notable highlight in the same period was in 1971, Brookfield Elks became the first team to represent Nova Scotia at the National Senior Men's Tournament in Halifax with the tournament games split between Halifax and Brookfield. The Elks finished 3rd overall, which was the best showing ever by a Maritime club led by the great third baseman Lyle Carter, outstanding shortstop Robert Putnam, and pitcher Cliff Surette.

From 1972-76, the Halifax League expanded to include the strong Fawcett's club out of Charlottetown, as well as Cape Breton and New Glasgow. For the Moosehead tournament in Halifax, teams were brought in from Quebec. As Speers recalls, "I believe the Fawcetts won one year, but that brings back another story worth repeating," he laughed:

> I got a call one evening from Tex MacDonald who asked if I could reschedule the Fawcetts' tournament game the next day in Halifax from 2:00PM to 4:00PM as there was an emergency. It seems that the outstanding Fawcetts' pitching ace Billy MacFarlane was having some difficulty securing his release from the big red hotel in Dorchester, New Brunswick. It was the first such request that I ever had to field. (Howie Speers)

The game was re-scheduled.

When the Fawcetts dropped out of the Mainland League,

Spears tried to recruit Tex for the Dartmouth Dairy Queen.
He opted to stay and play with his brothers in Charlottetown.
"I often wonder if I had been able to land Tex and Gerald
Fitzgerald out of Guysborough, two great power-hitting slug-
gers, we likely would have won the National Gold with the Dairy
Queen," sighed Speers.

Towards the latter part of 1970, however, Tex put together
his own team that could play and compete with any in the
Maritimes. Brothers Urban, or Rabbit, solidified second base,
Tex patrolled left field, Sandy, another dead fastball hitter who
could fly, played first base, while Sput played shortstop.

At this time, Sock was being groomed with Herbie's Smokies,
one of the lesser City League teams. The next summer when
Sock was ready, Sput moved behind the plate, and hard-hitting

*Fiddler Sr. throws out the first pitch to open the 1989
Charlie Ryan Baseball League at Charlottetown.*

Mike Flanagan shifted to right field.

On the baseball front at this time, Fiddler Sr. remained dedicated to the game he loved best and agreed to be manager of the 1975 PEI team headed to the National tournament that year in Winnipeg. Veteran pitchers Mike Kelly and Bill Weatherbie were outstanding, as was slugging young outfielder Marty Koughan, the Islanders surprised baseball Canada by earning a silver medal at the Nationals competition, the best showing ever by a senior team from PEI at that competition.

One of the more memorable events during this softball expansion occurred in July 1976, at Charlottetown's City Diamond when the strong Fawcetts' club and the Dartmouth Dairy Queens attracted a huge crowd of 4,000 fans for an exhibition double-header on both Saturday and Sunday. The Fawcetts won one of the four games and fans were treated to 11 home runs as Tex and Denny Clyke hit two each.

This was the same Dartmouth club that had lost the National title in the final inning later in the summer to Victoria Bates. At those Nationals, Tex and Clyke were both named all-Canadian outfielders, which helped cap a great year for the MacDonald family.

As the lights switched off on the 1976 season, it was another memorable one for our family: Jimmy Fiddler, Dad, was inducted into the PEI Sports Hall of Fame. The following year, it was almost a repeat as Tex earned All-Canadian honours at the Nationals in Hull, Quebec, the Sport PEI Senior Male Athlete of the Year, and the 1977 Lieutenant Governor's Award for excellence in Amateur Sport.

I immensely enjoyed watching my brothers win so many tournaments, and when not at the ball diamonds, started to spend time at the race track. Al McRae, owner of the CHTN radio station, hired me to do the race-day handicapping on his station, which paid bigger dividends later.

CHAPTER 10

A Big Win at the Race Track

ONE OF THE BEST DIVIDENDS, AND IT IS STILL PAYING out, did not require a bet. I met Gail Akerman. She was a single mom to four-year-old Lloyd, working full-time during the days as a secretary in the guidance department at Charlottetown Rural. On race nights—Monday, Thursday, and Saturday—she served at the Top of the Park at the Charlottetown Driving Park. We were married on October 31, 1975—Halloween night just like her parents during the Second World War—in St. Paul's Anglican Church in Charlottetown. While continuing my interest in harness racing, my new focus was in raising kids with Gail.

Instant family; rather than have Lloyd grow up with a name other than ours, I adopted him and he became Lloyd Frederick James MacDonald. In the mid-1980s, when he was old enough, about nine or ten, he enrolled in minor baseball in Charlottetown. His best friend was Bobby Drake. When Bobby was a year or two older, his father Floyd passed away suddenly, and with his mother very ill and hospitalized, Bobby moved in with us on a permanent basis.

My brother Sock coached Lloyd and Bobby with the Charlottetown Bantams and soon Bobby became a regular when the boys stayed in town at Mom's house, 87 Upper Prince, after baseball. Mom told me emphatically, "You and Gail take care of Bobby, and do not ask for any assistance from government or anyone; the good Lord will take care of you."

Bobby stayed with us from that point until he married to Patrice Ross, the woman we had picked out for him. Anthony and Mark were very young at the time, and Curtis and James were born after he came to live with us. Patrice, Bobby, and their son Alexander are important parts of our family. Patrice teaches Nursing at UPEI, and Bobby is the CDP blacksmith. Alexander attends Charlottetown Rural Senior High School. We travel together—we've been to Florida and Ontario—and attend all major family functions just as grandparents do everywhere. Patrice is very close to Anthony, Curtis, James, Mark, and Lloyd and their families. Bobby often goes to Ontario to help any horses with The Stable.Ca that require shoeing help. As the boys grew up, they always thought of Bobby as their older brother. They still regard him as such.

As for the good Lord looking after us, we are still here.

CHAPTER 11

Dexterity is the Macdonald Middle Name

AT THIS TIME, HUBERT "SOCK" MACDONALD HAD blossomed into a top-flight athlete not just in fastball and baseball but also in football. Canadian football proved popular across Canada, and the PEI senior high schools formed a very competitive league with the championship the Potato Bowl scheduled for every Remembrance Day, November 11. Many players graduated from the high school game to the Maritime university ranks. St. Dunstan's had competed in the Bluenose Conference, but, with the merger of St. Dunstan's University Saints and Prince of Wales College Welshmen in 1969, the University of PEI Panthers team was born. The popularity of the high school game was fueled also by the exploits of star running back Jim Foley from Ottawa, who starred with St. Dunstan's Saints and had developed into a solid performer with the Ottawa Roughriders and Montreal Alouettes of the Canadian Football League.

Sock picked up his love of football from our brother Tex, who had played with the St. Dunstan's High School Saints in the early 1960s under coaches Parker Lund and Tex. Tex was a tough running back, winning the 1963 Potato Bowl with St. Dunstan's High School led by star running back Les Affleck, who was by far the best running back in the province at the time.

UPEI 1980 Football Panthers: Front Row: (left to right) Coach Hillton, Mike Jones, Rick Kiraly, Sock MacDonald, Blaine MacPherson, Mike Lyriotokis, Dave Gauthier, Larry Currie, Gerald McKenna (Mgr.), Second Row: Tom Clow, Dave Bryant ,Dave Connoughton, Bill Bewes, Benji Stevens, Larry LeBlanc, George McGuigan, Carl Adams, Shane Foster (trainer); Third Row: Tom Corcoran, Chris Sullivan, Marcel Dupuis, Brian Thompson, Vernon Pahl, Kent Walker, Bobby LeClair, Jimmy MacInnis, Gerard Murphy (trainer); Fourth Row: Mike Kennedy, John Paul MacIntyre, Gary Kennedy, Danny DesJardins, Dave MacLeod, Mike O'Neil and Matty Colga.

After his university career, which included two years in anonymity in the backfield with Foley, Tex joined the Colonel Gray High School staff in 1972. He immediately took over one of his favourite roles as football coach with Chris Annett. Gray won the Potato Bowl that year, but lost in 1973 to Summerside as Gray's two top backs, Billy Fisher and Brian Thompson, were injured and unavailable after the first quarter of the Potato Bowl game. Gray went on to win in 1974 and 1975, thanks in no small part to rising star Sock MacDonald and a number of top Gray standouts such as Shane Dowling and Gary Kennedy.

All three joined Ed Hilton's UPEI football club, which boasted the best defensive club in Atlantic Canadian university play in this era. The addition of all-time great defensive standouts Mike Lyriotokis and Vernon Pahl, who later played with the Winnipeg Blue Bombers, made the Panthers a tough team to play against.

Sock joined the UPEI Panthers and earned 1975 Rookie of the Year honours, and for the next three years, was named Atlantic Conference Football all-star defensive back even though he played both offense as a receiver and defensive back. In his last year, he earned UPEI Athlete of the Year, and, in the off-season, was signed by the Montreal Alouettes. In late summer of 1980, after a solid training camp, he was the last player cut from the Montreal club that won the Grey Cup that year.

Today, the Potato Bowl on Remembrance Day is the prize for the PEI Tackle Football League as high school football was dropped in the early 1980s. UPEI football no longer exists but fall football is a big draw as Holland College has resurrected the football squad. Tex was the first head coach of the Holland College Hurricanes when they joined the Atlantic Football League in 2010. Holland College is also a major player in basketball, baseball, soccer, and their other athletic programs. They attract a large following and are well-received by the PEI business community.

While Sock credits Tex for teaching him the fundamentals of football, his success as an athlete can also be attributed to the genes he inherited from Jimmy Fiddler who starred in rugby during his university days in the mid-1930s at SDU. With football behind him, Sock returned to Charlottetown and starred and played in both fastball, with various clubs like the Fawcett's, the Sports Page, and Jody's Lounge, and baseball with the Morell Chevies of the Nova Scotia Senior League.

• • •

In contrast to the football league, the caliber of the softball league continued to grow reaching its apex when the 1980 Brookfield Elks earned the honour of becoming the first Maritime team to win the National Softball Crown.

The team demonstrated outstanding pitching and an air-tight defence that gave up just five runs in six national tournament games.

The great competition in this era prepared Brookfield for the Nationals, which is a greater feat for Brookfield considering the eligibility rules of the early 1980s. At that time, a player

CASEY'S LOUNGE - CHARLOTTETOWN, P.E.I.
NATIONAL SENIOR "A" MEN'S SOFTBALL CHAMPIONSHIPS
CALGARY, ALBERTA   AUGUST 25 - 30, 1987
BACK ROW - L to R: Steven Vaive, Mike Flanagan, Jeff Sheldow, "Sock" MacDonald, Don Sheldow, Keith Craswell.
MIDDLE ROW - L to R: Jack MacEachern - Manager, Sean Flanagan - Bat Boy, Blair McPhail, Tom McNally, Robbie Vessey, Dale Hickox - Coach, "Tex" MacDonald - Coach.
FRONT ROW - L to R: Gaye Hood - Coach, Jeff Hannam, Kevin Coles, Andy Worth, "Sput" MacDonald, Glen Gaudet, "Rabbit" MacDonald.

had to be a resident of the province as of June 1st to be eligible to play in the national tournament. Today, a provincial team usually is stacked with mercenary players from other provinces playing under a provincial flag only for the duration of the national competition. Additionally, a "national" tournament may have only representatives from five or six provinces.

By 1981, Sock had developed into the best player in the province by a country mile, the best hitter, and a short-stop blessed with sure hands, great range, and a cannon arm. He could also pitch and win at the national level, but taking him out of short-stop to pitch hurt the team until Keith Craswell came along. In addition, Sock was pitching more than he wanted simply because of the uncertain availability of ace Billy MacFarlane who was back at Dorchester. The bulk of the pitching load over the next four-to-five years rested not so much on Sock, but upon the shoulders of flame-throwing left-hander Jamie Lund who was loaded with ability and confidence. Sock, Mervin Power, and Joe Reardon had their moments at the Nationals while pickups Blair MacPhail, Pat King, Summerside's Allie Arsenault, and wily Covehead ace Freddie Morrison could be counted upon for good efforts. Morrison, especially, had the off-speed junk that gave big hitters fits. Whether the brothers—Sput, Sandy, Sock, Rabs, or Tex—played under Fawcett's, the Sports Page, or Casey's banner, one certainty was that this team could put runs on the board.

Perhaps another indication of the calibre of play exhibited in the Maritimes at this time occurred in the summer of 1981 when the Canadian National Fastball team toured the Maritimes. Since many of their players were from that hot-bed of fastball in Brookfield, they hosted two memorable double-headers. On a Friday night before 2,500 fans in Brookfield, unbeaten National team standout Robert Putnam went against unbeaten Jamie Lund. Fawcett's upset the National team and Putnam 2-1 in the opening game as both Sock and Tex scored the runs for Fawcett's driven in by catcher Sput MacDonald, who put on a show behind the plate.

In the second game, Fawcett's shelled Steve Healy, and jumped into a big lead only to lose in 12 innings 8-7 as Jamie Lund lost after six more great innings in relief of young Blair MacPhail. In this game, Sput threw out four would-be base stealers and homered, solidifying his reputation as one of the best catchers in the nation, while Tex blasted two long home runs; the last one forced the game into extra innings. Over the two games, pitcher Jamie Lund tossed 17 innings, giving up only 10 hits to Team Canada, an indication of how good the local team was in this era.

Jody's Lounge, with the MacDonald boys under Head Coach Eddy Power, knocked off the Tack Room in 1982 as Sock, Tex, and Sput led the way. Sock pitched both wins over their arch-rivals. The next summer, Sock played with Saint John Alpines in the New Brunswick League. He couldn't play on PEI because he was registered as a senior player in New Brunswick. Under new sponsorship of Casey's Lounge, I took over the coaching duties since Tex was not always available. He and his wife Melanie were expecting their first baby, and she was in and out of the hospital.

Without Sock, the task of defeating the Dairy Queen (previously the Tack Room) was tough but Casey's prevailed, knocking off the Surge Warriors in the finals as Sandy, Rabbit, Sput, Don MacLean, Stretch Gaudet, Avelino Gomez, and Mike Flanagan provided clutch hitting. In the championship game,

Butch Brown had a pair of key hits as the team won the right to attend the Nationals in British Columbia.

Summerside was and is a bitter rival for Charlottetown. In this era, the Summerside Caps, under Head Coach Roger Ahearn, also fielded highly competitive teams winning the right to go to the Nationals more than once. Ron Boland from Newfoundland was their pitching ace and they always had a solid attack with guys like outfielder Gerard "Turk" Gallant, Shannon Ellis, C J Gallant, Greg MacDonald, Hal Birch, Blaine Thibeau, and others. They went to the Nationals on a couple of occasions and usually picked up Sock.

The summer, however, produced the strangest play I've seen on any diamond. Subbing again for coach Tex, I took the Casey's Lounge team to a money tournament in Moncton where we advanced to the semi-final against Loggieville, NB. Once again Jamie Lund headed into extra innings in a close, low-scoring, one-run game with the winner to meet Saint John and Sock in the final game. In the Visitors' at bat and in extra innings, Loggieville's Jamie Watling rifled a line drive between our centre-fielder Don MacLean and right-fielder Mike Flanagan. All eyes were on the ball as Watling touched second base and turned towards third. To the utter astonishment of the few of us that saw it, our shortstop Don-Don MacNeil reached up and landed a perfect judo chop under Watling's chin as he spun out of control and sprawled on the baseline half-way towards third base. MacLean's throw from centre field was a perfect strike to third baseman David Gillis who easily tagged out the runner. The Loggieville bench went nuts. Umpire Ray Gibbs tossed a couple of their most vocal players out of the game as neither he nor any other officials saw what had happened.

At the 1985 National Softball tournament in Kitchener, catcher Sput MacDonald was named all-Canadian catcher. His hot bat with a powerful arm and great receiving skills earned an invite and a chance to play for the National team. He would have gone six or seven years earlier however, he had just started a new job with the provincial government, was newly married, and he opted to stay at home.

The boys continued playing together over the next few years, adding a sixth brother, Scott, who was an outstanding baseball pitcher in the senior ranks, but was making the cross-over from baseball at Memorial Field to softball at City Diamond. Scott had a live, moving fastball with a great bender. He pitched for Morell and Fort Augustus as a pick-up for the regional baseball tournament, but he didn't have the time to master the pitching game or the pitches in fastball. He was a sure-handed outfielder

PEI Provincial Senior A Mens champion Caseys Lounge head to the National Mens Softball tournament with five brothers in the starting lineup: Left to Right: Sandy MacDonald, Rabs MacDonald, Sput MacDonald, Tex MacDonald and Sock MacDonald.

and played with his other brothers, making six brothers in the same line-up, a feat never duplicated anywhere especially at the senior national level.

At the 1986 national tournament in Summerside, Sock emerged as the nation's top hitter. Tex earned national attention as his appearance was his 17th as a player, which tied him with Newfoundland standout Ross Crocker, a feat matched later by our brother Sock, with the most career trips to the Nationals.

Winning honors of any kind was certainly tough to do, because by this time, the talk of the softball world was Halifax-native Mark Smith who had vaulted onto the regional and national stage as a superstar, both as a pitcher and as a hitter. For the better part of the next 15 years, the game belonged to Smith as he dominated Canadian softball. Smith was the greatest-ever developed in this region, maybe even in Canada. He played for five provinces and in many areas of the United States in an era when the game was at its highest interest. At one tournament, his fastball was clocked at 109 MPH, which made him almost unbeatable when he brought his A-game.

In addition, Smith was a terrific hitter who could change the game as a pitcher or hitter. He pitched for Team Canada at the Pan Am Games, winning three Gold Medals, the last in 1991 before retiring in 1996. He was a great player in any era; the best Maritime pitcher of all time. It is not surprising that after his retirement, softball in the Maritimes suffered a sharp decline in popularity as baseball pushed softball into the background where it has stayed.

CHAPTER 12

Jack of All Trades

I ENROLLED AT UPEI AND GRADUATED IN 1975 WITH my brother Tex. Shortly after graduation, I was fortunate. Jack Hynes, who was Vice-Principal at Royalty Centre, lived a couple houses from our place on Upper Prince Street. He alerted me to the Student Services position at PVI, Holland College, Royalty Centre. I had the requirements: a License V PEI Teachers Certificate and people skills, and soon joined Holland College. In 1976, I accepted a position running the Student Services at Royalty Centre, and, from 1977 to 1987, I also taught upgrading at night school to the grade 12 level students in Charlottetown with Didi Wynne, Tom Corcoran, and others.

In those days, Royalty Centre offered students the opportunity of acquiring not only a valuable trade, but also of obtaining Grade 12-equivalent academic courses at the same time. A student spent a half-day in one of the trades such as carpentry, mechanics, welding, electrical, or clerk typist, legal or medical secretary, or cosmetology, and the other half-day at their home school. Students could attend full-time or part-time and, at the end of three years, the successful candidates walked away with a Grade 12 certificate and Block 1 of an apprenticeship program leading to a red seal trade certification.

Many of the students who completed moved out west where they could work as many hours as they wanted in their chosen trade, complete the required apprenticeship hours, and earn their certification papers. The school offered the best of both worlds and proved so popular and successful that students were bused into Charlottetown's Royalty Centre from Montague, Morell, and Souris in the morning, and from Colonel Gray, Charlottetown Rural, and Bluefield in the afternoon. This was a great opportunity for students who had no interest in university but knew exactly what they liked to do. Having a trade was just as good as having a university degree, better in many ways since trade students did not carry a hefty student loan. This opportunity should have been continued as it provided the Island businesses with tradespeople of all kinds and launched the careers of many successful business people.

Jack Hynes had just taken over as head coach of the UPEI Hockey Panthers on a part-time basis, and he asked me to help. John Neville, who had served as GM and started the Booster Club, had graduated (1979) and moved to Ontario with IBM, so Jack also asked me to help fill part or all of those roles. Jack had coached the famous Charlottetown Junior Islanders and the challenge to ice a competitive UPEI team was a daunting task. In addition to assisting Jack and his fundraising efforts, I decided to teach night school every Tuesday and Thursday at Birchwood where adults could upgrade their academic requirements for work advancement or for future employment. Looking back, I can tell you it was a very rewarding experience.

Holland College Royalty Centre also housed a number of very recognizable figures in Don "Hoss" Chandler, who served as Campus Administrator while Ev Stewart, the very successful North River Junior hockey coach, was on the teaching staff. Gerard Mitchell was also teaching before embarking on a legal career. Similar to today, the Panthers were always in need of money. UPEI's athletic teams have always been under-funded;

they were then and the same holds true today. As a result, the Booster Club also began a golf tournament to raise much-needed funds to assist in recruiting hockey student-athletes. Jack coached the UPEI Panthers from 1976-1983. Finances had reached the point where Jack's wife Marilyn made individual lunches for the players on road trips. Jack's teams were nationally-ranked numerous times and many of the players eventually played with the championship clubs of 1986-87 and 1987-88 under Vince Mulligan. Some of Jack's players worked at the race track as Jack operated the concessions in the summer months. Canteen workers were needed especially during Old Home Week, and one of the players who worked there was Trevor Crawford, a sharp-shooting sniper from Quebec who joined the hockey Panthers. Trevor played on a line with Gary Trainor and Callie MacPhail, and still holds the record for most goals—five—by a Panther in a single game. Ironically, Trevor's son Corey Crawford ended up not scoring goals, but preventing them winning a couple of Stanley Cups with the Chicago Black Hawks.

Jack's university clubs usually were anchored by four or five outstanding players and a sprinkling of solid two-way players. Former Quebec Major-Junior standout Wilf MacDonald was arguably the best defenceman to ever play at the university. He often logged 40 minutes a game. David Cameron, who jumped right out of the Island high school hockey league to star with the Panthers was another standout. Not surprisingly, Cameron landed in Colorado under GM Bill MacMillan, no doubt with a lot of help from Jack. Louie Lortier was another huge talent and I believe he won the scoring race in the Intercollegiate League. High-scoring Norman Beck also won a scoring race on a team that included talented Tony MacKenzie who scored 40 goals in a single season in the OHA. Other standouts were

clever Ron "The Artful Dodger" Carragher, brothers Dave
and Doug Currie, top two-way man Bobby MacDonald, Garth
Arsenault, and a pair of great defenders in Mike Ready and
hard-shooting defenceman Terry MacKenna. Avelino Gomez,
son of the famous thoroughbred jockey, guarded the pipes, and
was a colourful and sometimes outstanding performer.

Coach Jack Hynes is a legendary figure on PEI. He had
been offered pro hockey jobs from Bill Torrey of the New
York Islanders, but he refused because he was vice-principal at
Holland College. Jack had recommended Al MacAdam, Islanders
defenceman Gord Gallant and Peter Williams, as well as Hillard
Graves to the New York Islanders' GM, who realized that coach
Jack was a great judge of hockey talent.

Jack played a major role in Alan MacAdam's NHL career.
MacAdam started out with the Charlottetown Junior Islanders
under his coaching. In the 1968-69 playoffs, the Cape Breton
Metros were laying the muscle on the smaller Islander forwards
and on McAdam, who refused to take a retaliatory penalty. On
this night when McAdam came back to the Islanders bench,
Jack kept the gate closed. He ordered McAdam to march right
over to the Cape Breton bench and challenge his antagonist.
One of the bigger Metros quickly obliged but to the astonishment of Island fans, and likely Cape Breton followers, it wasn't
much of a fight. McAdam punched holes in his rival. From then
on, tackling McAdam on the ice was not advisable. He seldom
went looking for trouble but when it arrived, he was more than
capable of looking after himself.

New York Islanders' GM Bill Torrey and coach Jack had discussed when to draft MacAdam, so Torrey sent his head scout
to PEI to see him play.

The Philadelphia Flyers' scout was also on the trip. I don't know if they shared notes or not but on draft day, the Flyers signed MacAdam ahead of the Islanders, and he ended in the Philadelphia Flyers' camp. Fred Shero had liked MacAdam from the outset, but in the expansion draft the following year, he was forced to protect a higher-drafted player. This exposed MacAdam who was grabbed by Minnesota North Stars. In Minnesota, MacAdam flourished with a 42-goal season and a reputation as tough kid to tangle with. In the dressing room prior to one game against Minnesota, Shero offered these words of wisdom to his Flyers: "If you tangle with #25 [MacAdam], be first to fire and be ready."

Jack rarely is given the credit he deserves as a hockey coach, but MacAdam calls Jack "the greatest coach I ever played for." David Cameron, who also played for Jack at UPEI, eventually landed as a head coach in the National Hockey League with Ottawa, and coached the Canadian National Junior team as well. During his many years in the professional coaching ranks, Cameron often talked to Hynes during the winter months, feeling out his old coach on what he might try to make his team better. Cameron says that Jack "is the best coach I ever played for."

My second story involves Norman Beck who won the AUS hockey scoring race in his day. Beck could never be accused of being a defensive hockey player, and in many cases, most offensive standouts are not. Beck had loads of talent, could skate, and had a powerful shot, but blocking shots and checking were not part of his DNA. At a practice at the Old UPEI rink the night before a key playoff game, Jack insisted that all players participate in the checking drills. I asked Jack to exclude Beck

from the drill but to no avail. Instead of watching the entire
practice, I borrowed Jack's Thunderbird, and dropped into a
nearby watering hole for a couple pops. Upon my return, the
ambulance lights were flashing; Norman had missed a check
going over defenceman Brian Ostrowski and crashed into the
boards with what was thought to be a serious neck injury. The
moral of the hockey story; no checking drills for snipers.

Toward the end of the 1980s, Jack left Holland College
and took over the reins of the operation of the Charlottetown
Driving Park, the local racetrack where he was billed "The
Horsemen's Messiah" by owner Doug Hill. Jack had been a
horse owner since the days of the Junior Islanders and had
formed the Four-H stables of Harry Callaghan, Hynes, Len
Hookey, and Hilliard Graves, who had some success on the
stakes circuit. The horsemen needed a representative in dealing

UPEI Hockey Booster Club 1985 meeting: from left to right : Coach Hynes, Wayne Mac-
Dougall, Dr Harry Callaghan, Fred (Fiddler) MacDonald

with CDP owners Doug Hill, Duck Acorn, Mel Jenkins, and Bill Hancox, as meetings had begun about the horsemen securing the track from the present owners. When the deal was finalized in 1990, Jack took over as General Manager and changes were soon in place.

When Ed Waters resigned and stopped calling the races at the CDP, the hunt was on for a new track announcer. In my Saturday sports column, I wrote that they didn't have to go far because I had heard a young man calling the races in a bar one evening after closing hours and he was terrific. He had a great voice, was quick to respond and funny: Kevin "Boomer" Gallant. Boomer went on to fashion a great career as an announcer and later as the CBC meteorologist. He's also considered one of the greatest race callers in this region.

Jack and Boomer formed a terrific duo. They worked tirelessly in making Old Home Week, which is the cornerstone for the Gold Cup and Saucer, a success, bringing in horses from off-Island, especially from the USA, Ontario, and Quebec. Jack also needed Maritime horses to fill the Old Home Week cards. Since I had been a race secretary in Fredericton, and knew a great many of the people involved in racing in the Maritimes, I helped Jack in this area. In addition, I wrote for both The Guardian and The Atlantic Post Calls helping to promote harness racing and the CDP. Gail worked as a photographer, and took over that role at the track. Our boys soon followed, but at different posts.

CHAPTER 13

The Making of a Politician: Tex MacDonald

THE MACDONALD BOYS WERE NOT MUCH INTERESTED in politics, and, after watching the backroom boys in action in a by-election in 1972, I could not recommend the game of politics to anyone. Popular historian and author David Weale contested the 5th Queens nomination leading up to the 1974 PEI General election. He was up against veteran Conservative party organizer Jim Lee. I worked for David securing delegates for the various polls and lining up enough of our delegates, hopefully to win the right to represent the Conservatives in that important Charlottetown riding. The by-election was held at the Basilica Rec Centre, and David delivered a tremendous speech of his vision for the well-being of the province. Jim's speech was acceptable and skillful but far from David's performance. I could sense the vote was extremely close; Dr Harry Callaghan confirmed this later.

At 7:30PM, the polls were supposed to be closed for voting. Situated at the front of the hall, I was watching the clock closely, with my attention on the back of the hall where I could see who was coming and going. At about 10 minutes after the polls were supposed to be closed, I noticed three of Lee's supporters, Diddles Doyle plus Toby and Alan MacDonald, enter and vote. I can guarantee that they did not vote for David. I believe that those votes provided Lee with the margin of victory. I thought then and I still do that had those late three votes not been allowed to count, David would have won the nomination. The final tally was not released.

I am certain that Lee would not have had anything to do with it or would play unfairly, but sometimes over-zealous workers do get carried away. Jim Lee went on from there to be Premier of the province, but I often wonder how the political landscape would have looked had David Weale won that nomination

During the provincial election, Mom worked and voted for Jim Lee, but I'm not certain Dad did because he was very secretive about his voting. Everybody knew for certain that Mom voted for Lee but Dad, who was set in his ways, liked Addie MacDonald who was running for the Liberals in what was then 5th Queens. Dad often talked about the "Scottish clans," which suggests to me that he voted Liberal.

• • •

The little-boy games such as fastball, baseball, football, and hockey invariably end. On PEI, the big boys play politics, an exciting and dangerous game for which Tex was inadequately equipped. His popularity took him a long way, but his devotion to political life and party policies, which was only skin deep to begin with, was a game plan destined for trouble. As political commentator Eugene Rossiter quipped during one of Tex's early political campaigns, "The people that will vote for Tex are 'Texans' and therefore not likely to vote along party lines."

Like everything that Tex ventured into, it was full speed ahead: In 1987, that approach worked well with municipal politics. While he was still teaching at Colonel Gray, Tex first contested the Charlottetown counsellor's seat in Ward Five, and again in the next civic election when John E. "Spy" Ready won the Mayor's seat in 1988. The easy victories in the rough and tough political playground may have come too easy. It seemed as if the victories led him to believe that perhaps he was unbeatable in the city.

In those days, Spy was also the Manager of the Basilica Rec Centre, from where he planned his political campaigns—after hours of course. Tex and I, with Stu MacFadyen, worked two nights a week managing the bowling alleys and operating the nightly bingos. The three of us filled in and took turns as night managers if Spy was away doing military training in Aldershot, Nova Scotia, or at various hockey meetings. In the fall of 1988, Spy suffered a heart attack and his wife Anne called and arranged for the three of us to work for Spy until he recovered.

In 1992, Tex ran for the mayor's chain of office and won, upsetting sitting-Mayor Ready. During his two-term tenure from 1992-98, his stay at City Hall was marked by a number of positive initiatives. He helped bring the professional PEI Senators to the city and also played a key role in the amalgamation of Sherwood with Charlottetown, thereby enlarging the tax base. He fought for more money from the province, insisting that the city grant was disproportionate to the revenue that the government earned. In his second term, the strength of his personality led to a smooth transition of police, fire, and essential services in the amalgamation period. He was also a driving force on the completion of the boardwalk around the perimeter of the waterfront, which is highly popular with Islanders and visitors. Confederation Landing Park was another project near to his heart.

We all enjoyed Tex's meteoric rise in politics; Mom especially was so proud of him. She was particularly pleased the day Tex was sworn in as Mayor, although some of his political decisions brought her plenty of turmoil. She was not one to hide her feelings on some of his decisions and she had no trouble telling him so. When George MacDonald upset Tex for the Mayor's seat in 1998, Tex was convinced, against Mom's advice, to run for the Conservatives in the following provincial election with running mate Ron MacMillan against Joe Ghiz and Paul Connolly. They were no match for Joe Ghiz who, by this time, had become a major player on the Canadian political scene and an extremely popular figure on the Island.

Eventually, Tex and the Conservative executive parted ways and he jumped to the Liberal Party where he was considered a strong city candidate in the next provincial election. As a candidate for the Liberals, he likely would have won had Leo Broderick not entered the fray making the contest a three-party race, taking just enough votes away to spell defeat for the Texman. In sports, Tex had the timing of hitting a baseball or softball down cold. In politics, where timing is also everything, he discovered that timing was quite different from sports. After an unsuccessful run at the Liberal leadership, won by Keith Milligan, he ended his political career as a candidate.

Historians will have different opinions about Tex's political career, but they can't write that it was boring. Had his political career been managed right, and had he picked his spots wisely, he could have had a longer stay on the political stage. However, Tex did things his way: no excuses necessary.

Tex returned to Colonel Gray as a guidance counsellor, but he couldn't get politics out of his blood. He joined forces with Robert Ghiz, who was contesting the Liberal leadership, and delivered a huge youth vote at a convention where the voting age was 16 years of age. It was this youth vote that carried the day and, in a hotly contested convention, that factor tipped the scales ever so slightly in favour of Ghiz over Alan Buchanan. When Robert Ghiz won the 2007 provincial election and became Premier, he looked after his Colonel Gray buddy, appointing him Executive Assistant to the Premier.

Another of Robert's first decisions as Premier was the appointment of Sandy MacDonald, now armed with his PhD, as Deputy Minister of Education under Minister Doug Currie. This was a tumultuous time in Education with school closures and rebellious public forums; however, the province could not have picked a more capable and astute leader than Sandy who is a bright and gifted communicator. Sandy stayed almost to the end of the Ghiz years, before moving from government to Holland College as Vice-President. On January 6, 2019, he was appointed President of Holland College, the second native Islander to hold the position, Alex MacAulay being the first.

As a politician, Tex was likeable, charming, and approachable, and it was for those very traits that both Conservative and Liberal politicians pursued him as a candidate; ironically, those same traits may have contributed to his political downfall. His two-term, five-year tenure as Mayor and his contributions to the city and the province are areas that he can look back upon with pride and satisfaction. Today, Tex is a highly popular and entertaining figure in the city, an able organizer and hard worker who spends most of his summer days playing golf at various

Island courses including Avondale, his home course. When asked about politics today, he shakes his head and has a good laugh.

CHAPTER 14

Behind the Glass and Doors of Hockey and The Guardian

IN MY ROLE IN STUDENT SERVICES, JUNIOR HOCKEY teams often approached me to find full-time courses for the players that they had recruited. Most players had their sights set on professional hockey, but some were interested in careers in the trades such as electrical, plumbing, carpentry, welding, or autobody. Most of the requests for a spot in a program came after the school year had begun so finding a course with available space was not that easy.

In October 1986, Sherwood Parkdale Head Coach Stevie Gallant came to my Royalty Centre office hoping to secure a place in one of the trades for a Newfoundland hockey player named Darren Langdon. Nobody in Charlottetown knew much about Langdon, who had played senior hockey the previous year on the Rock. The junior hockey camps here had been going for about three weeks, and registration for Holland College classes was on September 8.

There were no spots open in any of the trades, so I decided to ask Newman Wight, the welding instructor to see if he could do Stevie a favour. I hoped that he would take Langdon, so I reminded Newman that it was likely one student would drop out before Christmas. Taking Langdon was not an outrageous request. Newman, however, was not interested in Steve's problem. When Stevie Gallant suggested that he would secure three or four hockey sticks for Newman, who was still playing recreational hockey in Georgetown, the situation brightened. I indicated that I would look after his class a couple of Friday afternoons so he could leave early, and that finalized the deal. I had no idea that it would set off a powder keg with Sherwood Parkdale's bitter rivals, the Charlottetown Abbies.

Gallant, who had played and fought his way through the Newfoundland senior ranks and the Herder Cup, had heard from some of his Newfoundland buddies that Langdon was a rugged customer. Stevie was more impressed when he was shown video of Langdon thumping all of the tough guys in the NL senior league. Within the week of seeing the video, Stevie landed in my office telling me how happy he was that "we" had secured a spot for Langdon.

Two weeks earlier, Abbies' Head Coach Forbie and GM Jim Kennedy had come to my office trying to secure a spot for Ray Skinner and another player. Previously, the Abbies' management had been able to secure placements in the various trade programs; however, neither player was interested in our full-time programs nor were there any other spots available. On the other hand, Langdon promised to attend every day and was interested, which was a different situation than that of the Abbies' players.

Stevie, who had been married to Forbie's daughter, was behind the Sherwood Metros' bench. Langdon's arrival and "special" treatment made it worse. "Your own mother is a director of the Abbies, and here you are helping that bunch in Sherwood," was the usual greeting to me from Jim Kennedy in the early days of the junior league that winter.

What Stevie had neglected to tell me was that he had no money for Langdon's course or meals as his team was just getting off the ground. When I found out, I immediately helped Langdon fill out his student loan papers and sent them to the proper authorities in Newfoundland.

As time went on, Holland College's finance department located at Charlottetown Centre contacted me weekly to ask why Langdon's student fees were not paid. I informed them that as soon as his student loan arrived, the matter would be resolved.

At that time, Holland College Royalty Centre operated a cafeteria service and many students from Charlottetown Rural Senior High, less than 200 yards away, came up for the hot meals at noon time. Since neither Stevie nor Langdon had much money, I arranged with cafeteria manager Sylvia MacInnis, who previously looked after Griff's Diner across from the Charlottetown Forum, to feed Darren but charge him half-price since he could eat at 12:30PM, when the prices were lowered. The plan was to pay the bill when Darren's student loan money arrived.

A month or so later, we received correspondence from Newfoundland but no money. Since Newfoundland offered the trade in their province, the government would not be providing any funding for Langdon. Almost in tears at the news, Stevie asked if I could do anything. Naturally, he didn't want to lose Langdon, who by this time, had beaten Forbie's long list of very capable individuals like the McCabe boys, Ray Skinner, Bert Weir, and Sean MacInnis. And the fights were getting longer and meaner.

I contacted Hillsborough Member of Parliament Tom MacMillan, who resolved the situation and arranged for

Langdon to get the student loan. When the money arrived, Langdon, without being asked, walked over to Sylvia to pay the entire bill, but she charged him $100 and called it square. Langdon was a person of great character. The next morning Jim Kennedy was at my door again complaining that I had helped the enemy Steve Gallant and the Metros, and that I worked against my "mother and family friends," and the Abbies' executive. I reminded Jim that welding was a trade that the Abbies' players were not interested in. That didn't matter to Jim. From that day until the rest of the year, I was banned from the Abbies' dressing room as a writer.

Every game that year between the Abbies and the Metros featured a Langdon fight and he won just about all of them decidedly. The Friday night Abbies' home game packed the Forum, and every Saturday morning, Mom's place on Upper Prince was crowded with family and friends going over the Friday night fights and games: my brothers, Shane Dowling, Paul Gormley, Pork MacRae, Mike Quinn, Gary McGuigan, Mike Kennedy, and UPEI hockey coach Vince Mulligan.

One of Langdon's regular dance partners with the Abbies was rough and tough Sean MacInnis, who unfortunately passed away a few years ago. Sean lived at Mom's place during the hockey season, and just about every Saturday morning, he had a souvenir from Langdon: A closed eye, a black eye, a facial cut, or a fat lip. Sean was not deterred. "One of these nights, it will be my turn," laughed Sean and he kept on trying. He was a game and rugged lad, a crowd pleaser, and a gladiator who was loved by the Charlottetown fans.

The next season, the Metros folded but Langdon, who had turned out to be a useful hockey player at the junior

level, besides being the best enforcer in the province, joined
Summerside Western Caps, a provincial and another enemy of
the Charlottetown Abbies in every sport, but especially hockey.
It was a year like the previous season: night after night, the
Abbies were after him, and night after night he answered the
bell. When he finished his junior career, Langdon played in the
Eastern League and American League before joining the New
York Rangers in 1994-95. He stayed in the NHL until he retired
after the 2005-06 season. He is back in Newfoundland with
his wife and four kids, the most successful Newfoundlander in
NHL history. He is remembered best on PEI by Stevie Gallant,
the Sherwood Parkdale hockey supporters and the Kennedys.

• • •

With the hockey season over, the sports scene on the Island
shifted to fastball, baseball, and, one of the most popular sports,
harness racing. The Gold Cup and Saucer was and is one of the
major races in North America, usually drawing more than 15,000
people for the August race. The 1986 Gold Cup and Saucer race
was, as usual, staged on Friday night. Wanting to keep the huge
crowd on the Island for another day or two, organizers toyed with
the idea of moving the big race to Saturday night, but decided
not to make the move for one more year.

Don Morrison had just begun what was to be a long and
highly successful career as a Guardian writer and, most impor-
tantly, as The Guardian's Sports editor. He was very knowledgeable in all PEI sports except harness racing. However, The
Guardian and Patriot editor, J. Pius Callaghan, publisher Bill
Hancox, and race track owners Duck Acorn, Mel Jenkins, and
Doug Hill, were very interested in maximum coverage for the
Gold Cup and Saucer. J. Pius asked me to take Donnie under
my wing for harness racing at the CDP.

J. Pius informed me a few days before the race that this was to be the last Friday night Gold Cup and Saucer race, and that I was responsible for getting the feature front page story to Donnie immediately after the race in time for the Saturday morning edition of The Guardian. Donnie was to stay back at the office, finish the layout, and leave the proper space for my special on the Cup and Saucer. As The Guardian had been in union struggles with the typeset people and other workers,

J. Pius wanted everything to run smoothly, as in no overtime, because Saturday was a key edition.

With only the standard phone line, the chances of getting a call through to Donnie late on the Friday Gold Cup and Saucer night were highly unlikely. The race had finished by 11:30PM, but by midnight and 12:30AM, there was still no story for the front sports page and The Guardian workers were getting restless by the minute.

After fighting my way through the race crowds and traffic… Well, I suppose I had a few beer and a bite to eat at the Winners' Stable at the CDP barn area, and just like that it was after midnight. I walked from the track to The Guardian on Prince Street, maybe a ten-minute walk. On the way, I was putting the column together in my head. I finally arrived at close to 1:00AM. Donnie was almost in tears. "Both of us will likely get fired over this and the union guys out back were sure to be in contact with publisher Hancox over this matter," lamented Donnie. The coverage was splendid; at least, that's what J. Pius told me. To my surprise, I received only a mild scolding as he and publisher Hancox were delighted with the pictures and story. I can still see Donnie putting on his jacket around 2:00AM and lamenting, "this should never happen again."

When he joined *The Guardian*, Donnie Morrison had a full head of hair. Within the decade, the locks had almost disappeared. Moving the Gold Cup and Saucer race to the Saturday night was much easier on him as he had Sunday afternoon to put the sports pages together, and keep his editor and publisher happy.

CHAPTER 15

Barry Ling, the Fight Doctor

BOXING SELDOM IF EVER MAKES *THE GUARDIAN*
sports pages these days, but back in the late 1980s and early
1990s, professional boxing was making a final stand on PEI.
In the 1950s, 1960s and 1970s, pro-boxing cards were staged
at numerous locations: at the Charlottetown Forum or in
Summerside, Montague, or Victoria. Fighters such as Harry
Poulton, the McCloskey brothers—Tom, Cobey, Ace, and
Wilf—Don "Duck" Trainor, Gaston Roy, Peanuts Arsenault,
Jim Poulton, and Tiger Steele had a strong following. When
top-notch visiting fighters were brought in, crowds often hit
the 2500-3000 range. Tom McCloskey went on to train some
of the greatest names in Maritime boxing history, fighters like
Canadian champ Richard "Kid" Howard of Halifax, Cape
Breton's Blair Richardson, another Canadian champ Buddy
Daye, and future world champion heavyweight Trevor Berbick.

Over the past 25-30 years, numerous attempts have been
made to revive the sport of boxing on the Island with guys like
Howard Watts and Joe Borden, both of whom had success with
their pupils in the amateur ranks. The last good professional
fighter to come from PEI was the under-rated Don Boulter of
Victoria who fought and competed against some high-ranking
opponents. By the late 1980s, Boulter had fought on cards in

Charlottetown, Summerside, Crapaud, and Montague; however, his major bouts were outside this region in United States and Canada.

As a *Guardian* writer, I decided to cover a boxing card featuring local Kevin Vuozzo against a Halifax fighter at the Montague rink. My brother Tex, family friends Tom Corcoran and Robert "Greasy" Gallant, as well as the official ring doctor Barry Ling and his friend Roy Scantlebury, two of the more colourful characters to grace the PEI sports scene, were along for the ride. We met at the old fire hall at the back of City Hall next to the Rodd Charlottetown, and headed to Montague with more than a few pops aboard, which seemed the thing to do in those days. Barry was the ring doctor that night and all the way down to Montague, Roy told everyone that he hoped we'd see a knockout.

Sure enough, Roy got his wish in one of the early preliminary fights: a quick knockout, and the referee summoned the ring doctor. Dr. Barry jumped into the ring to attend to the stricken fighter. Unaware that Scantlebury had meddled with his doctor's black bag, Barry reached into his pouch and pulled out a large industrial flashlight—strong enough to brighten that entire section of the arena. So powerful that the light frightened the wobbly fighter who, by this time, was coming to his senses. Roy had also removed the small rubber reflex hammer and replaced it with a large claw hammer, and when Barry pulled it out of his bag, the ringside fans and the referee burst into laughter. Within seconds, the fighter climbed to his feet, took one look at Barry, and shuffled back to his dressing room. Dr. Barry looked to where we were sitting, and all he could do was shake his head and laugh.

Earlier that evening, Greasy Gallant, who was a standout junior hockey player with Sherwood Parkdale Metros, was having his own problems. He had been with us near ringside and watched as a fighter was taking an eight-count, and with one hand on the top rope, he caught Greasy's attention and winked at him. Greasy responded by throwing popcorn at him.

Security rushed over, grabbed Greasy, and ushered him out of the arena. He entirely missed the main event.

Later that summer, Barry was the main character in a story that landed him in the QEH as a patient, not as a doctor. Barry loved harness racing and hockey, and he played a prominent role in both sports from the time he first arrived on the Island after his graduation from Dalhousie Medical until his unfortunate passing in 2010. He thought of himself as a top harness racing driver, especially when he had a few drinks aboard. One summer afternoon, he convinced his talented CDP trainer-driver Paul MacDonald to take him to the matinee races in Pinette where he would show what he could do in the bike. That afternoon, everything was going along as planned: Barry in Paul's colours astride a horse that he thought couldn't lose especially on the tight Pinette half-mile track. Heading into the final turn of the race, the horse refused to turn, reared in the air like Silver in the Lone Ranger, and tipped over backwards on top of the good doctor. Barry's ribs were broken and he was sent to the hospital.

Barry, an orthopaedic surgeon, was Chief of Surgery at the QEH. He always encouraged his boys Jamie and David, and his daughter Suzie, a nurse at the QEH, to be the best they could be. He was a major player in minor hockey, with both boys as junior hockey standouts, David was Major Junior Player of the

Year in Canada while in the OHA, and eventually made it to the National Hockey League, while Jamie starred in USA university hockey. Barry was also a kind and generous guy making sure children who could not afford skates or gear got what they needed by paying out of his own pocket. He was one of a kind.

CHAPTER 16

Diamonds are a Boy's Best Friend?

BRIAN LEWIS APPROACHED ME IN THE SPRING OF 1986 about coaching the provincial champion Charlottetown Junior Legion baseball team with him. It was great to get back into baseball. We had a good junior team with pitchers such as Dave Hippy MacDougal, Nick Nicholson, and hard-hitting Norman Beck. Unfortunately, the Maritime junior final didn't material-ize that fall. Yet, the experience told me that should the oppor-tunity ever arise again to help teach the kids something about the game, I would do just that.

In the early 1980s, baseball was enjoying a resurgence on the Island thanks to the Kings County League and to Forbes Kennedy, who had kept baseball alive in the city through his association with the senior Regal Oilers, and Orin Carver, with both advocating for a senior league. Many other people were involved, such as Charlie Ryan, Dave LeClair, Mike Kelly, Wayne MacDougall, Don LeClair, my mom Pat, and Vern Handrahan, who formed the executive of the new Charlie Ryan Baseball League. No doubt the success and popularity of the Toronto Blue Jays and Labatt President Don MacDougall from Ellerslie, PEI, played a huge role in baseball's growth and popularity right across Canada.

During the winter, organizers of the Charlie Ryan Senior Baseball team made plans for a draft of all the players interested, although the Regal Oilers entered their own team with Forbes Kennedy. Vern Handrahan handled the Investors' Club with Jim Hogan as unofficial manager. Dr Bob Lund was named President of the League, and baseball returned to Charlottetown's Memorial Field in a league like the popular one of the 1950s.

The next year, the teams were put together according to sponsors with the Regal Oilers, a heavily stacked team with the Roche boys Albert and Everett, Dave MacIsaac, Bob O'Shea, Ron Kline, Blair Creelman, and others. Jim Hogan spearheaded the Investors' team under Vern Handrahan; they had a couple of top pitchers in Gordie Roche and Andrew Davies. Gilligans sponsored George Gregory and Jack Gay, and later Bob MacMillan sponsored the Sports Page Club, which I handled. We finished in a tie for first with the Regal Oilers. We had ace left-hander younger brother Scott, veteran Willie Koughan, a terrific money pitcher and hitter, plus hard-hitting speedster Marty Koughan, and catcher Phil Gorvette. The League proved to be very competitive and successful. My two boys, Anthony and Mark, also became interested, and played minor ball in Charlottetown much to Granny Pat and Fiddler Sr.'s delight as they got to see them play.

The next summer in 1989, I took over as Head Coach of the Canada Games Juniors in the Charlie Ryan League. We finished in first place by a wide margin. However, we were not permitted to play in league playoffs since they started the week we were in Saskatoon for the Games. Baseball was back in the province, and from that point on, interest in baseball far exceeded softball for fan support. The 1989 Canada Games'

The 1986 Charlottetown Legion Junior baseball team:
Coaches Brain Lewis and Fred MacDonald, white hats front row.

experience was filled with wonderful memories made more delightful since I liked GM George Burke, and we had a solid club. In addition, my brothers Tex and Sock were in Saskatoon the entire Canada Games Week: Tex as Mayor representing the City of Charlottetown, and Sock representing the corporate Moosehead Breweries.

I was confident that the PEI team could score runs with guys like first baseman Thane Arsenault, slugging catcher Thane Hughes, brothers Paul and Ian Power, David Gillis, Dwayne MacDougall, and outfielders Alan Plaggenhoeff, Ron LeClair, and Matt Beardsley. We had right-handed pitchers Glen MacKinnon, Dave Cullen, and Joey Carroll; they could throw hard but had limited pitching experience. We were well prepared, working every night teaching proper cut-offs, how to defend against the bunt in sacrifice situations, and when to switch defensive coverage. We had very smart middle infielders in Gillis and the Power brothers, which helped a great deal. This extra defensive work paid off immediately as we won the opening game against a very good Newfoundland club.

On offense, I wanted speed at the top of the batting order, a guy leading off that could fly, would take strikes, and not be aggressive until the count was full. Matt Beardsley was just the boy. Additionally, he was a top outfielder with a great arm. Switch-hitter Ron LeClair had the two-spot, was a good hitter, would make a pitcher work, and could fly as well. First baseman Thane Arsenault was a terrific hitter, a little on the Hollywood side, but with great hands although his arm was weak. Talented catcher Thane Hughes was next, followed by a trio of excellent

Canada Games 1989 Baseball standouts Ian and Paul Power with Head Coach Fred MacDonald

hitters in Power brothers plus hard-hitting Al Plaggenhoeff, all of which gave us as good an attack at the Canada Games as anyone.

In the opening game at the Games, our work on defending paid off. Newfoundland trailed 8-7, but had the runners on first and third with one out. They were at the bottom of their order eight and nine, two left-handed hitters, while we had hard-throwing Glen MacKinnon pitching in relief. We had watched all their hitters early in the game and were confident that neither could pull a MacKinnon fast ball. We switched responsibility and had our shortstop play the hitter, a left-handed hitter, and the second baseman cover the bag. Then the hitter hit a hard liner right at our shortstop who threw to first for the double-play and the ball game. Hard work, practice, and knowing what to do sometimes pays off.

However, at the end of the tournament, we were in the hunt for a top five finish but bad luck came our way. We were ahead of Nova Scotia in a pivotal game with a 3-2 lead and we had the sacks full. Thane Hughes rifled a shot between the outfielders that cleared the sacks giving us a big lead. As Ron LeClair rounded third heading for home, I looked at the base umpire who was watching the ball in the outfield when Nova Scotia players started calling that LeClair missed the bag. I had watched him touch the inside corner of the bag but the umpires got together, called him out, and we lost the game in extra innings. It was a brutal call. We ended up finishing 2-3 and we should have been 3-2. Glen MacKinnon won two games at the Canada Games and not many can say that.

In 1991, the PEI Canada Games team had a top left-handed pitcher in Niall Hughes who had played for my junior team when he was 15. He had loads of talent and at the Games, he impressed, although his PEI team could not score any runs for him. The Los Angeles Dodgers' scouts loved what they saw and signed him to a pro contract. The 1991 team also would have had the best positional player on the Island by far in Sandy Shea, but the young man from Tignish didn't get a chance to go because he could not get to all the practices in Charlottetown or Morell in eastern PEI. Shea had tremendous power, speed, and a great throwing arm, certainly one of the three best in the province regardless of age.

In 1991, my Sports Page Senior team headed to St John's, Newfoundland for the Atlantic Regional Senior tournament. We had a tune-up game at Memorial Field against Tignish on a Sunday. The PEI team had an Open card, which meant we could add a player for the Newfoundland tournament. I

Young horsemen Anthony MacDonald, extreme left, and brother Mark, extreme right, join Maritime great driver Dave Pinkney and Fred MacDonald after harness racing promotion at Truro Raceway.

hadn't seen Sandy Shea playing before. He impressed me. That afternoon, Shea homered, made a couple of excellent running catches, showed a great throwing arm, and could fly; an exceptional track guy in high school. We had an extra card open for our Sports Page club and, during the game, Richard McGuigan of Bulldog Construction visited our dugout. He asked us if we had room for Shea on the trip, and I told him yes, but we had no money remaining. Richard bought his ticket, and Shea was off to the Newfoundland tournament.

In his first game in Newfoundland, Sandy hit a home run for us, a blast into the wind that impressed my old buddy, Mike Buist, who was headed the next day to the Summer Games out west representing Newfoundland. How anyone could leave this

Two legendary PEI baseball figures get ready for the first pitch to open the 1989 baseball season at Memorial Field, Charlottetown: Charlie Ryan and Fiddler MacDonald.

talent back on the Island is hard to believe but on PEI it happens, too frequently for me. Sadly, that evening Sandy fell down the stairs after that dazzling first game and was lost to us for the remainder of the tournament. It was left to another Tignish native to star in this tournament: hard-throwing right-hander Spencer Myers picked up one of our wins going the full seven innings. They grow them tough in Tignish.

We were 2-3 at the 1991 Nationals in Newfoundland beating Dartmouth Moosehead Dry, but in the three-way tie for third, Dartmouth advanced based on fewer runs allowed.

Over the next three years, our team played at the National Senior Men's division in Moncton, Quebec City, and Kentville, always winning a game or two despite not having any pitching depth, which was needed in a regional or national tournament. The nucleus of the '89 Canada Games baseball team led the way as I expected—guys like Thane Arsenault and Thane Hughes were great hitters as were the Power boys, Ian and Paul. We also added a mix of top senior players like veterans Hippy

Sports Page Head Coach Fred MacDonald at Memorial Field, Charlottetown.

MacDougall, Marty Koughan, Willie Koughan, Dave McIsaac, Ron Hennessey, catchers Gerry Campbell, Phil Gorveatte, and Craig Conohan.

In this senior era, Newfoundland had the best overall pitching staff of any of the Maritime clubs, and, in my view, should have won a national title with that staff. Newfoundland always had great pitching in baseball or fastball, and this can be attributed to American Air bases in that province and better minor baseball coaching. In the Atlantic regional tournament in 1993 in Moncton, I remember a conversation with Moncton Mets' Head Coach Ralph Chambers who told me that since Moncton was the host club, they had the option of which club to face on opening day.

The Mets felt they did not want to face PEI's two lefties Blair Creelman or Paul Affleck, but when I told him Gary Furlong, Frank Humber, or Darren Colbourne were better than our two guys, he was more than concerned. Ralph hadn't seen Furlong in Kentville the previous year, and the lefty from Grand Falls was again over-powering, blanking Moncton on two hits and 12 strike outs.

Nevertheless, the players who played on my PEI teams until the mid-nineties remain my friends, so there's more involved here than wins and losses. As they got out of baseball to pursue their non-sport careers, I figured it was time for me to get out of the game. My boys were playing minor baseball in Charlottetown and falling in love with the harness racing game.

CHAPTER 17

Granny Pat to the Rescue

WHEN WE MOVED TO KINGSTON, JUST WEST OF
Charlottetown, in the late 1970s, we purchased a house plus
five acres from Harold Godfrey with the hopes that one day the
boys might be interested in raising a horse of their own. That
would have to wait a while since Lloyd and Bobby were in senior
high, and Anthony and Mark were too young for horses and
wanted to play baseball in Charlottetown. Unfortunately, there
was no organized baseball in Kingston. However, we were only
8.7 miles from Mom's place on Upper Prince, so in the early
1990s, the boys spent many summer days with Granny Pat who
enjoyed taking them to the ballpark.

At 12, Anthony was tall and lean, had great form as a pitcher,
could throw hard, and had plenty of raw talent. Yet, he wasn't
the best listener. Additionally, while he liked playing baseball,
he'd rather be at the race track, which didn't go over well with
his baseball coaches. On the other hand, at 10 years old, Mark
was small for his age, feisty, and willing but not strong enough
to be an impact player. The boys often travelled to the race
track where Gail was the track photographer taking over from
her friend Sharon Carver who had a full-time government job.

Anthony's baseball coach, Jack Matheson, told me where
Anthony and Mark may be headed. Coach Matheson informed
Anthony that he'd be pitching in a little league tournament in
the afternoon during Old Home Week, and Anthony told him

without consulting me that he would not be available because of the afternoon races. Anthony and Mark would often be found on race track splitting tickets and hanging around some of the horsemen. Anthony befriended veteran Wendell Ford and started helping him while Mark was a regular on race days at Garry MacDonald and Lenny Myers Stable both smitten with the harness racing bug. Within a few years, both wanted a horse of their own, perhaps a mare at home would be a good idea and maybe they could raise a horse of their own.

While Anthony and Mark were playing Little League, Mosquito, Lloyd and Bobby Drake were playing Bantam-Midget also at Charlottetown and the coach was my brother Sockie who somehow found time to handle this group. Bobby (who we unofficially adopted) was the ace pitcher and catcher and one of the best players, but he had a hot temper, which endeared him to Sock. Lloyd was a second baseman with limited range and ability, and as I told Gail, "he's no Rabbit."

Lloyd was destined for the race track as well since he was an "IT geek" and was interested in producing the Charlottetown Driving Park in-house show, which had been started by Dr. Don Ling and Norman Hall. Lloyd's grandfather Lloyd Ackerman was a radar specialist in the Air Force and his daughter Gail inherited those skills and passed them on to Lloyd. Along with Bobby's help, Lloyd started LFJ productions and soon Greg Blanchard came aboard to act as host for the show, which produced the first Old Home Week nationwide telecast when Jack Hynes was General Manager at the Charlottetown Driving Park.

Anthony and Mark had spent a great deal of time at 87 Upper Prince Street often staying over and keeping Mom company as did Lloyd and Bobby. Mom had insisted that Lloyd and Bobby finish their grade 12 at Bluefield and go to university, a career path that she demanded of all that lived under her roof. As expected, both graduated with academic standing at Bluefield, Lloyd was off to university, and Bobby off to blacksmith school as he too had fallen in love with the harness racing game.

Mark was the first to try the matinee tracks as every Sunday morning beginning when school was finished late June 1994, veteran horseman Cecil MacDougall, who lived down on the Cornwall Road, would arrive at 11:00AM at our place in Kingston to pick up Mark and head to the races at St. Peter's Matinee track, which is no longer in operation. Clifford Affleck, now a judge at Red Shores Charlottetown and Summerside, put the races together and he usually had enough horses for eight races with four or five in every race. It amazed me how Cecil made it to St. Peters as the truck seemed frightfully low to the ground with the two horses aboard. Gail and I with Anthony, Lloyd, and Bobby usually travelled to St. Peters a little later but always on time to see Mark drive; in those early days he wore the colours of Len Myers. Mark won two races that opening matinee day with both of Cecil's horses.

Prior to the matinee track experience, Anthony and Mark spent more time working actively at the racetrack than I ever did; my experience was gained watching Wally McInnis and the Hennessey clan working with the horses in their care. Wally worked for Don MacNeil, one of the best horsemen in the region, jogging the horses, cleaning the harness, and most important putting them away at night after the races in a clean stall with plenty of water. Wally also picked up pointers on how to do the job right from his uncles who looked after the

Greenbrier horses and from another uncle, meticulous care-taker Ralph "Boo" Shepherd.

Growing up right in the heart of the city, the MacDonald boys—mostly Tex, Sock, Sandy, and me—had seen Joe Hennessey take care of horses at the Peake Street lane barn as in those days, horses could be stabled in the city; however, Charlottetown by-laws, enacted in the 1970s brought an end to that practice. We also raced at the CDP on the road parallel to the backstretch in the evenings just as we did on the Peake Street lane. Part of the learning experience also included looking for tickets. On race nights, and after every race, we looked for discarded tickets under the grandstand and sometimes we found "good" tickets thrown away by tourists or by patrons who did not understand the "stable" concept whereby two horses could race as a stable and if either one came 1st, 2nd or 3rd the patron would still cash. In July and August when the tourists arrived, this concept proved too much for tourists and "good" tickets often were discarded—resulting in a nice pay day for some of us. We were more interested in gambling and betting, but Mark and Anthony were much more interested in driving and training horses.

I should mention here that we learned how to care for horses and how to jog from the Charlottetown race track caretakers in the 1960s, who took the time to show us the anatomy of the horse, various ailments, and how to get them back to the track safe and sound. Richard Bradley was one such trainer and he was extremely knowledgeable about horses, sports, history, politics, and life in general. He took me under his wing and advised me on all horse related matters. He finished Grade 10 in the all-boys Queen Square school but he was and still is one of the smartest guys I ever met. Richard worked for Roach MacGregor here on PEI and in the USA, and later for about 25 years with the legendary Stanley Dancer; he and his partner Peggy Bishop supervised the Little Brown Jug paddock on Jug Day until 2010 when ill health forced him to the sidelines. Another youngster that Richard took under his wing from Ohio was Jason Settlemore, who is the GM of The Meadowlands in New Jersey and one of the sharpest young men in harness racing.

Two others that Richard introduced to the sport of harness racing at a very young age are my brothers Sandy and Sock. Sandy worked for one summer as Richard's caretaker while Socky and Wally Hennessey worked that same summer for John "Buddy" Campbell.

I knew Anthony and Mark had gotten the harness racing bug and I was not surprised when Mark arrived home from Bluefield one day and told me he wanted to try a career in harness racing. I told him that I'd call Mike MacDonald at Blue Bonnets, a great family friend and the next day he was on a truck with Ron Gass to Blue Bonnets in Montreal. Within six months, Anthony would join them at Blue Bonnets and, as Mark said three years later, "Anthony and I graduated from Mike U." They found out from Mike how to handle people and how to care for horses, lessons from a man who ran a first-class professional stable. They are forever grateful to Mike for their careers and both were painfully upset with Mike's passing in June 2018 in Charlottetown.

While Anthony and Mark were starting their harness racing careers with Mike in Montreal, Lloyd was expanding his LFJ Production team while moving into his third year in business at UPEI. Eventually television production and "the tech field" became a fulltime venture as he joined forces with Sydney native Bruce Gaum of Dome Productions. Dome and Lloyd produced many Gold Cup and Saucer races for the national audience and Bruce was so impressed with Lloyd and his little brother Curtis that he moved them to Blue Bonnets to handle the simulcast operations there. Dome eventually hired Lloyd and Curtis to help produce the World Junior hockey tournament and the World Curling Championships from Halifax, Nova Scotia.

Within a year, Lloyd went on to oversee the Sky Dome in Toronto for Bruce while Curtis stayed in Montreal. It was during this stint at Blue Bonnets that Curtis met with Simon Allard who became one of his closest friends. Curtis convinced the Allards to come and race in the Gold Cup and Saucer, and two years later, the Allards parked their trailer in Kingston, PEI, to find out in person what the Gold Cup and Saucer was all about. Curtis credits his relationship with Simon for his ability to speak French and, as Simon said often last summer, "he speaks fluent French but only when he's drinking beer."

Mark stayed with Mike and worked for him at Blue Bonnets for two years and when Mike shifted to Windsor Raceway for a winter meet, Mark moved with him. After the winter at Windsor, Mike decided to return to Montreal and Blue Bonnets, but Mark decided that he would break out on his own. He came back to PEI briefly, picked up some horses from owner Neal Moase and headed back to Windsor in the fall of 1998. The three-legged pacer Notenoughfunds and the top mare Slay the Devil won consistently, and his success caught the attention of top Canadian trainer Bob McIntosh and his career took off.

Anthony also moved to Windsor and, shortly after, to Hazel Park, Detroit, for Tom Wine. Within the year, he returned to Montreal where he posted his first win with Careys Pride, April 5, 1998, and enjoyed success with Maritime-bred trotter Absolute Proof.

Both Mark and Anthony were very close to their grandparents, especially Fiddler and Pat; unfortunately, there were difficult times ahead back on PEI.

CHAPTER 18

Losing the Foundations

"I'M NOT A YOUNG MAN ANY MORE," SIGHED FIDDLER Senior in his new home at Whisperwood Villa on St. Peter's Road. The move was necessary, not for health reasons, but for Mom's fear that Dad might burn down the house on Upper Prince. He often left cigarettes smoldering in the strangest places: near the couch, the end of the table, or the bathroom. It's difficult trying to convince seniors to move out of their homes and into a residence that's specifically for older folks. Dad was tougher than an axe-handle to convince.

"There doesn't appear to be any semblance of romance at this stage of their lives," I commented to Gail. It was sad to see this happen after all those years of their togetherness. The age gap of eight-to-ten years between Mom and Dad began to play a role as they grew older and further apart, not exactly a healthy relationship for anyone at their stage of life. Whatever the cause, by 1996 Dad was calling Whisperwood Villa "home," and in time he grew to enjoy the facility, which was beautiful and only a few minutes from anywhere in Charlottetown.

We all visited Dad at Whisperwood. He especially wanted me to visit on Saturday mornings in the hope of getting to the races in the afternoons during the long winter months. He enjoyed it more when I took him a few 50mls miniatures of whiskey, which he relished. After a couple of minis, he'd be all set for the race track in the afternoon. My boys, Anthony and Mark, loved to visit Grampy and they would also take him to the races every chance they could.

One morning after downing three or four minis, he persuaded me to take him to the track where we'd have a few beer and talk to the people that he knew. His memory was showing no sign of fatigue. He often told me, "There is nothing wrong with me whatsoever. Your mother wanted me to move to Whisperwood, but I'm fine now." Numerous people came in and out of the bar those days, and Fiddler knew almost all of them, reminding me of a story or two about each as the day wore on. He bet every race, won some, lost some, and continued sipping the beer. At the end of the race card, it was a chore to get him to leave. I'm certain he would have stayed longer had the management not enforced the last call. On many occasions, Anthony drove Dad directly back to Whisperwood against dad's wishes because he wanted to stop for a nightcap.

One Sunday after a long Saturday at the races, Ebby Devine visited Fiddler at Whisperwood and later phoned me with his analysis of the visit. "Your father seemed a little confused and out of sorts when I visited him this afternoon," moaned Ebby. I told Ebby the rest of the story, and his old goose hunting buddy felt much relieved given the complete story from the trip to the racetrack.

The stay at Whisperwood was not without its more humorous moments. One morning I got a call from dad and he informed me that we had to go to Ernie Duffy's funeral that morning. I was to pick him up early, go to lunch at the Sportsman's Club, and then attend the service at MacLean's Funeral Home just across the square from the bar. Dad and I headed over to Ernie's funeral, seated about the middle near the aisle where

Dad could have an unobstructed view of the proceedings. Dad's sight was fine, but his hearing left a lot to be desired, which meant he often spoke louder than normal to compensate. "Where's Ernie," Dad lamented as he looked around and couldn't see the casket. I could hear the chuckling around us, so I gave Dad the "shush" sign of a finger in front of the mouth. He didn't get the message. At the end of the service, the family moved towards the back of the Funeral Home. Still not able to see the casket, Dad blurted out loudly, "Where's Ernie?" "He's in an urn," I explained. Dad replied in a voice that all could hear, "Ernie's in an Urn?" It was the last funeral that he and I attended together while he was still alive.

In many ways, his life was successful despite the difficulties of the war and the stress of raising a very large family. He was a scholar, very well read, a gifted writer, and a top-notch athlete. After his playing days, he relished the exploits of his sons and daughters, which gave him enormous pleasure although he seldom showed it on the outside. He was inducted into the PEI Sports Hall of Fame in 1976, and since 2005, the Charlottetown Mosquito AAA team have held an annual tournament in his honour. James Leslie "Fiddler" MacDonald died January 6, 1996.

Dad's passing was the second in two years for the family. Bonnie, Dad's favorite of the girls, was a busy person. She managed various retail operations, such as clothing stores and lounges, including The Page at Rodds and Caseys on University Avenue, which sponsored the softball team. She also managed bars and lounges in Alberta and British Columbia. She had a great sense of humour and enjoyed her wine and beer. Bonnie was not athletic like Ramona or Peggy but she was the family's biggest fan and had followed the boys in many of their national fastball tournaments throughout Canada. She also took her holidays at the location of the senior men's softball national tournament. Bonnie was killed in a car crash in British Columbia in 1995. Her loss was painful.

The Charlie Ryan Baseball League and its executive, which included guys like Mike Kelly, Wayne MacDougall, Dr Bob Lund, David LeClair, and of course our mother Pat, held a pre-season meeting on Sunday, May 4, 1997, at Colonel Gray High School. Mike Kelly, one of the greatest athletes ever developed in this province, stayed for most of the meeting but left early as he wanted to catch the ferry. He was representing the province at a meeting in Moncton with Atlantic Canada Opportunities Agency the following morning. We didn't see Mike alive again. He died on May 5, the following Monday morning, which brought an early and unfair end to a great athlete and person. He was only 50 years old. Mom and I attended Mike's funeral in Morell.

Five weeks later, on June 16, Mom was expected to attend a Saturday afternoon baseball game at Memorial Field. When she didn't attend, I knew something was wrong. I got to the racetrack at 6:30PM. Rabbit met me and told me that Mom had suffered a heart attack. We immediately took off for the hospital. She was not in good shape when we went to visit again briefly Saturday evening. Sunday afternoon, she lamented to me, "I want you to phone Bernadine and tell her not to bother coming home. I'm all right." I was not so sure. I saw terror in her eyes.

The next afternoon, Monday, June 19, 1997, she passed away suddenly. Mom had been the glue that kept the family together all those years. Where Dad had been passive, she brought fire and passion to the dance. In almost all cases, her words of wisdom rang true. Her death changed all our lives completely. I read once about a doctor in a troop ship off Saigon during the hectic days of the Vietnam War. What stuck in my mind was what the doctor said: "In the depths of the hospital ship where young men lay dying or recuperating from lost limbs and the like, almost all invariably in the moments of darkest despair, they cried out for their mothers." Losing Dad was a terrible experience, but losing Mom was, I guess, even more painful for us all.

Mom had loved my boys unconditionally, and was especially happy when they came to visit or stayed for the evening. I hadn't learned to appreciate grandchildren but now I cannot live without them. The day that Mom took her heart attack was the day that Mark won his first lifetime race at Rideau Carleton Raceway in Ottawa. She was so happy with Mark's first win even though she didn't have long to enjoy it. I can only imagine how proud she would have been at their eventual success in harness racing. She certainly would have been proud seeing Anthony, Mark, and James all racing against one another in the 2011 Gold Cup and Saucer.

CHAPTER 19

Chasing the Gold Cup and Saucer

BY THE TURN OF THE MILLENNIUM, MOM AND DAD were gone, Tex was out of politics, and my boys were just beginning their racing careers in Ontario. I had hopes of raising a horse in Kingston, and sending it up-country, most likely to Anthony since he was training, driving, and breaking colts. That was considerably different from Mark who was strictly a catch-driver. Being a city boy, I didn't know anything about breeding horses or farm work, but I did enjoy studying pedigrees. I joined one of the early PEI Select Yearling Sales committees with Richard MacPhee, John Furness, Brad Murray, Bob Connolly, Erwin Andrew, Dr Blair Kelly, Ralph Annear, and Jack Bernard. I had my eyes opened to this aspect of the harness racing game.

The first sale I participated in as a director was the third annual Select Yearling Sale held at the Kennedy Coliseum, September 15, 1977. It featured yearlings by sires like Newport Robbi, A C's Dandy, Adios Alex, Yankee Timer, and a few trot sires such as Call the Roll and Cyrano. The Yearling Sale was a new venture for our group, and the quality of the stallions and of the brood mares was modest compared to the stock in this region today.

When Gail and I first moved to Kingston 40 years ago, I got the feeling that the neighbours must have had a laugh or two at the novices from the city. We both had a great deal to learn about country living in all seasons. On a very hot summer day, I noticed Hubert Proud and his wife—our next-door neighbours—loading the hay wagons for storage in the loft of their big barn right next door. Gail suggested that I should lend them a hand and help him with the haying. That would be the proper thing to do. I arrived wearing short pants, a golf shirt, and a ball cap. No long pants or clothing for me; those people were not too smart wearing long-sleeve shirts and pants on such a hot, muggy day.

I arrived home at dusk about six hours later, exhausted and cut to ribbons. Another lesson learned the hard way. I think that, year after year, I continued to keep the neighbours on their toes. I am certain that they were in stitches with laughter watching the city boy stacking hay in short pants and a golf shirt. Although nobody brought it to my attention. I suspect Clifford, Donna, Richard and Nick Green, Willard and Hubert Proud, Leith and Wayne Newson, Michael and Sue Doyle, Blake MacDonald, the hockey expert Garth Holmes, and Don and Harold Godfrey and sons all heard about it.

On our first winter in Kingston, I didn't bother banking the house or worrying if the house was properly insulated. Although Kingston was just about 8.7 miles from mom's door on Upper Prince, or 15 minutes on a bad traffic day, during that first winter when many of my pipes froze and burst, I thought about going home to Mom. What a mess.

Another neighbor H. B. Willis and his wife Annie lived about a mile further up the Kingston Road. He had a well-maintained racetrack on the corner of the Kingston Road and the Colville Road, a horse farm that included prize cattle. I had often visited the farm, and he and his wife Annie liked to have little visitors like Anthony and Mark come over to watch top horses in training. In his day, H. B. was a big player in North American harness racing with horses like Arnie's Aim, fourth in the 1981

Islanders in the Little Brown Jug winners circle after Mark MacDonald's victory with pacer Mr Feelgood in front of 50,000 fans at the Delaware county Fair, Ohio. Pictured from left to right: Bob Whitlock, Fred MacDonald, Shawn McIsaac, Steve Dunn, Ron Carmichael, Dennis King, (2020 PEI Premier), Rabs MacDonald, Pat Dorsey.

Mark and Mr Feelgood get to the wire in world record 1:50 in Little Brown Jug.

Hambletonian, Primo Hanover who raced in the Maple Leaf Trot, and Sing Along and Yankee Predator, 1984 Invitational winner at The Meadowlands.

H. B. was the only Maritime owner ever to race a horse in the Hambletonian. He also co-owned the pacer Meteor Hanover, who raced in the biggest pacing event in North America, the Little Brown Jug, with Billy Rix. Besides Meteor Hanover, there were other top pacers that trained on the Willis track including Canu Bay, Matrix Hanover, and Pearle's Falcon for trainers like Alex and Ricky MacPhee and Lee Taylor. H. B. and his partner Billy continued their search to find a Gold Cup and Saucer winner to the very end, but with no luck. Ironically, one of the horses that H. B. owned but sold was Pearle's Falcon who came back to win under other ownership.

When the boys were very young, I bought Glengyle Roxy with Billy Rix and, although she was a stake champion in the Maritimes and raced at Mohawk in Ontario, the Dominion Byrd mare did not throw anything special. Another lesson learned from this experience was that a mare's success on the racetrack does not carry over into success in the broodmare ranks. Momma didn't have to be a big money winner; far more important was the pedigree and the history of the family. Conformation and pedigree most often are far more important in the breeding business than speed records.

After Bobby had graduated as an academic student from Bluefield, he spent time learning the blacksmith trade in Texas. He then decided to give the horses a try in Ontario, working for Callie Rankin both training and as a blacksmith. At that time, I was looking for a mare by Brisco Hanover, which would cross perfectly with any son of Speedy Crown. Within a month, we landed Rau D Judy, 2:02:1, from a very successful family. The same family that produced Highland Lullaby t, 1:58, Tentative Deal t, 1:59 and Latest Chapter t, 3, 1:55:1. The fourth dam was Cassin Hanover, one of the great foundation mares in the trot world. Bobby brought her back to PEI, and the following year, we decided that she would be a promising broodmare.

She was that and more: Island-owner Boyd White purchased her second foal by Whiteland Somolli. She took a record of 1:56:4, banked $199,000, and earned Aged Trotter of the Year at Cal Expo in California for Rocky Stidham. Rau D Judy also produced The Big Fred, time 1:56:4, who was sent to Anthony's stable at Campbellville, Ontario. The Big Fred was good enough to win the $72,000 Molson Trot at Georgian Raceway and bank $298,000 lifetime, while taking a 1:56:4 record, although he was charted in 1:54 and change at Mohawk and Woodbine. In his big win at Georgian Downs, Anthony was blocked most of the way, but he somehow found room on the outside and stormed home for the victory, and a $36,000 slice of the purse.

Broodmare Rau D Judy also has to her credit the very fast Ontario Sire Stake Gold winner Duke MacCallum, time 1:56:4, who beat the A trot colts in Ontario, and showed closing quarters in 26 and change. He could fly but a bad ankle prevented him from being a great colt. In winning at Woodbine towards the end of his career, he made a break leaving, spotted the field 20 lengths, and still won with something to spare in taking his lifetime 1:56:4.

Our first broodmare in Kingston, Glengyle Roxy, produced Atlantic Sire Stakes A placed Jimmy Fiddler by Major League. Stratosphere, another mare owned by Jack Hynes, produced Dusty Lane Blue, one of the few horses to beat Kilkerran Fury in his three-year-old campaign. Without question, the best pacing broodmare was Easy Consent, owned by Harold Arthur MacInnis, who worked for Jimmy Doherty at Foxboro and later Meadowlands. Art had started out at the Charlottetown track in the mid-1960s with Buddy Campbell. They had one of the best stables in the Maritimes with horses like Hi Jay, Amos Frost, Stormy Song, and Lola Hal, the horse that gave Art his first lifetime win at the CDP in 1967.

As for Easy Consent, she stayed with us until she was 29, passing away just before Christmas 2017. Her first foal was the mercurial Victor Laszlo who won his Provincial Cup Trial in Saint John beating the likes of Six Day War, and stepped to a lifetime best of p,1:56:3, his final quarter in 26:3. Owned by Kansas Snow of Sydney, and campaigned by the talented Roddy Jamieson, Victor Laszlo raced in the Gold Cup and Saucer Trial but hit the starting gate leaving and missed the final.

● ● ●

H B Willis was like many other prominent Maritime horse owners that tried throughout their lifetime to win the coveted Gold Cup and Saucer. In major league sports, athletes strive to win the World Series, the Stanley Cup, or the Super Bowl; for Maritime harness racing fans, the big prize is the Gold Cup and Saucer. Since 1960, we have watched the Gold Cup and Saucer grow in stature from being the top invitational race in the Maritime Provinces to a plateau reserved for the top races in Canada and among the "must-see" races in North America. James "Roach" MacGregor was the first to bring outside horses for the race when he arrived here with Dr. Harry C from Rockingham and Foxboro to capture the 1967 Gold Cup and Saucer. Bringing in horses of that caliber attracted harness

YEAR	HORSE	DRIVER	TIME
1960	Dee's Boy	Lloyd MacAulay	2:06
1961	War Cry Ranger	Elmer Smith	2:06:3
1962	Dee's Boy	Myron MacArthur	2:06:2
1963	Bob Brook	Walter Craig	2:04:3
1964	June Byrd	Jim MacGregor	2:08
1965	Andy's Son	Jimmy Moore	2:07
1966	Andy's Son	Jimmy Moore	2:04:1
1967	Dr Harry C	Jim MacGregor	2:04:3
1968	Miramichi Post	Joe Goguen	2:05:3
1969	Firebolt	Art Porter	2:05:3
1970	Firebolt	Art Porter	2:03:4
1971	Andy's Son	Elmore White	2:05:1
1972	Prince Abbot	Wayne Whebby	2:05:1
1973	Dr Walter C	Les Waite	2:05:4
1974	Scotch Gauman	Bill Nicholson	2:04:4
1975	Ventall Rainbow	Mike MacDonald	2:04:2
1976	Power Baron	Mike Doyle	2:01:4
1977	Ventall Rainbow	Mike MacDonald	2:08:1
1978	Nickname	Phil Pinkney	2:02:2
1979	Kaweco	Henry Smallwood	2:02:4
1980	Saul's Pride	Joe Smallwood	2:03:3
1981	Henry Butler	Steve Mahar	2:00:3
1982	Saul's Pride	Joe Smallwood	2:00:2
1983	Silent Class	Marcel Barrieau	2:01:2

1984	Pearl's Falcon	Mike MacDonald	2:02:2
1985	Winner's Accolade	Mike MacDonald	1:57:3
1986	Rev Your Engine	Phil Pinkney	2:02:1
1987	Gimble	Paul MacDonald	1:57:4
1988	The Papermaker	Ian Moore	2:01:2
1989	Stargaze Hanover	Harry Poulton	1:57:3
1990	Tigerbird	Mike Downey	1:58
1991	Portent	Doug Brown	1:56:1
1992	Kilkerran Ingle	Emmons MacKay	1:56
1993	Little Black Book	Paul MacKenzie	1:54:1
1994	Nuclear Flash	Mike Saftic	1:55:3
1995	Sandy Hanover	Mike MacDonald	1:56:1
1996	Tough Hombre	David Smith	1:54:4
1997	Comedy Hour	Gilles Barrieau	2:00
1998	Native Born	Brett Robinson	1:53:3
1999	Order to Go	John Holmes	1:58:2
2000	Canaco Simon	Gilles Barrieau	1:56:3
2001	Scarlet and Gold	Wally Hennessey	1:54:1
2002	London Mews N	Gilles Barrieau	1:53:3
2003	Sand Oils Dexter	Mark MacDonald	1:53:2
2004	Sand Oils Dexter	Mark MacDonald	1:55:2
2005	Driven to Win	Wally Hennessey	1:51:2
2006	Banner Yankee	Carl Jamieson	1:54:1
2007	Silent Swing	Phil Hudon	1:52

2008	Pownal Bay Matt	Earl Smith	:53:4
2009	All the Weapons	Ken Oliver	1:53
2010	Part Shark	Scott Zeron	1:51
2011	Blissful Breeze	Mark MacDonald	1:53:1
2012	Eighteen	Tyler Moore	1:51
2013	Escape the News	Marc Campbell	1:50:4
2014	Bigtown Hero	Brad Forward	1:50:4
2015	Take It Back Terry	Marc Campbell	1:50:4
2016	Y S Lotus	Lou Philippe Roy	1:50:1
2017	Shadow Place	Gilles Barrieau	1:50:1
2018	Somewhere Fancy	Simon Allard	1:50:4
2019	Rock Diamonds N	Mitchell Cushing	1:51:4
2020	Time to Dance	Marc Campbell	1:51:4

racing fans not only from Atlantic Canada but also from the major markets in North America. This is thanks to the originators of the event, men like Doug Hill, Mel Jenkins, Bill Hancox, and Duck Acorn for having the vision to launch the race with glitter and glamour, including reference to the horses and girls in silks in the Gold Cup and Saucer Parade, aspects that set this race apart from all others in North America harness racing.

• • •

The first of the boys to gain prominence in the Gold Cup and Saucer, but not as a driver, was Lloyd who joined forces with Greg Blanchard to produce the television show at the racetrack under the LFJ Productions handle. The first in-house show was produced by Norman Hall and Dr. Don Ling. When they dropped out of the picture, Lloyd and Greg took over. Today, Greg is the Director of Racing at Western Fair, London, ON, and is often an analyst for many of the major harness racing events from Canada and the United States. Lloyd has a successful refrigeration business in Ontario, but finds the time to assist Curtis, the fifth boy of our blended family, and his wife Jaimi with the Open House telecasts associated with The Stable.ca, and with telecasts from The Cavendish Beach Festival.

Mark was the first of the boys to compete in the Gold Cup and Saucer, which he did after an apprenticeship with Mike MacDonald at Blue Bonnets. He and Mike moved to the Windsor Racetrack for the 1999 winter race meet. There, Mark's career blossomed. He was the leading driver at Windsor Raceway, winning the driving title in 2000 and 2002. In the process, he became the first driver to surpass $1,000,000 in earnings in a single season at Windsor. The following season, he moved to Western Fair winning the leading driver award there as well.

Mark returned to PEI in August 2003 to contest the prestigious Gold Cup and Saucer with Western Fair-based pacer Sand Oils Dexter. He won it in dramatic fashion catching Harmony P and his mentor Mike MacDonald right at the wire. Mark repeated the win in 2004 with Sand Oils Dexter. He tried for three-straight, but the horse wasn't healthy enough to turn the hat-trick even though he won his trial.

Mark had gotten off to a faster start than most drivers, including Anthony, posting 695 wins in 2005, a Canadian record at the time, and the first PEI-born driver to do so; that year, he won his first O'Brien Award as Canada's leading driver, the only Islander to achieve such a feat. The following year, Mark posted 745 wins and was the leading driver on the Woodbine-Mohawk circuit while winning his second O'Brien Award presented to the leading Canadian driver.

In 2006, Mark captured the 2006 Little Brown Jug at Delaware, Ohio winning consecutive heats with Mr. Feelgood for trainer Jimmy Takter. For a young kid from PEI winning the "Jug" was a huge accomplishment joining Joe O'Brien as the only Islanders ever to visit the Delaware, Ohio, Little Brown Jug winners' circle. As a parent, being there for both events was extremely exciting.

2006 Little Brown Jug Chart

1 Mr Feelgood (Mark MacDonald)
2 Cactus Creek (Mike LaChance)
3 Armbro Deuce (George Brennan)
4 Total Truth (Ron Pierce)
5 Texas Shootout (Yannick Gingras)
6 Armbro Dynamic (John Campbell)
7 True North (Dave Palone)
8 Western Ace (Brian Sears)
9 Doonbeg (Jody Jamieson)

Time: 1:50:3

While Mark had positioned himself among the top drivers, Anthony was doing double-duty training and driving horses while gaining a reputation as a talented developer of young horses especially trotters. He posted his first lifetime win aboard

Carey's Pride at Blue Bonnets in 1999 before claiming and winning with a Maritime-bred horse Absolut Proof, a trotter and a gait that Anthony still prefers to drive. He wasn't afraid of work and persevered with his modest stables at Belleville and Peterborough in Ontario. He graduated to the Mohawk, Woodbine and Flamboro circuit in the early 2000s; again, it was his work with trotters that established him in Ontario. Trotters like An Angel for Earl and The Big Fred (1:56—$298,000) who won whenever it seemed that Anthony needed a win, kept food on the table in a very competitive industry. He raced a competitive group of stake horses like Say Nyet, sophomore trot standout, and drove Surrealist to a 1:55 victory in the $180,000 OSS three-year-old colt event at Kawartha Downs in October 2008, beating a top field that included Stonebridge Terror.

By 2007, Anthony's stable at Campbellville had grown to 65 horses, but he was working himself to death. He gradually reduced this to a more reasonable number. He had success with trotters like The Big Fred, numerous OSS stake-winning trotters, while travelling back to PEI for the August Gold Cup and Saucer. One of his top pacers at that time was Noble Tess for Sydney-native Bruce Gaum who came to contest the 2003 Gold Cup and Saucer. Anthony has returned to promote and compete in the Gold Cup and Saucer race almost every year since then.

Anthony has had his share of tough luck in the Gold Cup and Saucer: he was fifth to eventual millionaire-pacer Silent Swing with Presidential Kid in 2007. That same week, he established a Charlottetown record for three-year-olds with P. H. Jackpot (1:52:4), which still stands. He was a fast-closing third with Panda Bear to Part Shark and Scott Zeron in the track record 1:51 mile in the 2010 classic.

In 2011, Mark was back to contest the 2011 Gold Cup and Saucer. That occasion was quite different as his two brothers Anthony and James drove against him; the first time such a scenario was seen in a major race on this continent. It was also the first time in Gold Cup and Saucer history that three brothers competed against each another in the race.

Gold Cup and Saucer 2011, Purse $60,000
Three MacDonald brothers in Gold Cup and Saucer, first time ever.

1 Blissfull Breeze—Mark MacDonald
2 Firethorn—John MacDonald
3 Part Shark—Gilles Barrieau
4 Western Ace—Mike Stevenson
5 Pontiac Luck—Robert Shepherd
6 Fleet Sensation—James MacDonald
7 Oakmont—Danny Romo
8 Did It Again—Simon Allard
9 Fire on the Water—Anthony MacDonald

Winning Trainer: Dean Nixon, Owner: Les Racicot, Ontario

Time 1:53:2

While winning a Gold Cup and Saucer has always been on the minds of Anthony and Mark, it was rarely on the mind of their youngest brother James. More interested in hockey, baseball, and golf, James was recruited by Georgian Downs' GM, Chris

Roberts, to work in the marketing department after taking the program at Holland College in Charlottetown in 2007. Shortly after going to Georgian Downs, the horsemen and the track could not reach an agreement, and a strike ensued putting an end to racing until a contract was reached between track and horsemen. Not wishing to return to PEI, James joined Anthony, who was training a big stable at Campbellville Training Centre, now the Tomiko Training Centre. James loved the training and the excitement of racing, and he soon ditched the marketing idea and moved to working with the horses full-time. He won his first race with Ricky MacPhee's Tough Luck during the 2008 Old Home Week.

Meanwhile, Anthony continued his quest for a Gold Cup and Saucer victory during Charlottetown's Old Home Week. He came so close that on one occasion Red Shores' announcer Lee Drake, positioned at the wire, called Anthony the winner. This was the 2015 classic when Anthony was pushed three-deep on the turn and roared up on the outside to miss by a nose with Atta Boy Dan. In that one, Marc Campbell hung on to win with Take It Back Terry. The previous year, Anthony won his trial with Stonebridge Terror in 1:52:2, but lost in the close final to Eighteen who went a monster mile for Tyler Moore and owners Serge Savard Sr., Ian Moore, and R G McGroup.

In 2016, Anthony drove Limelight Beach in the $60,000 Gold Cup and Saucer final against the likes of Foiled Again, but it was not to be as his horse did not fire as Y. S. Lotus went gate-to-wire for driver Louis-Phillipe Roy and trainer Rene Allard. In the 2018 race, Anthony was listed to drive his horse Lincoln James, but when the Saturday night race was postponed, he had to leave for a USA stake race and Kenny Arsenault drove in his place.

For the past five years, Anthony's career has really blossomed as he and his wife Amy successfully launched the fractional ownership group The Stable.Ca, the biggest harness racing stable in Canada and one of the biggest in North America. A passionate speaker about harness racing and fractional ownership, Anthony has been asked to speak at just about every major harness racing jurisdiction in North America as the popularity of The Stable.Ca continues to grow. In addition, the governing bodies of harness racing in Australia and New Zealand invited Anthony to speak on behalf of fractional ownership "Down Under" and he completed a two-week, multi-track tour of both countries, culminating in the start of a The Stable.Ca operation in Australia which has already produced stakes winners.

While Mark and Anthony have been putting their mark on the sport, James has been solidifying himself as one of the top drivers on the Ontario circuit for the past decade. In 2019, he posted the most dramatic victory of the season in a major race when he rallied from off the pace to take the $500,000 Canadian Pacing Derby with Courtly Choice at Mohawk in 1:48 and change, upsetting the great Lather Up and returning a hefty $98 for a $2 win ticket. The previous summer, James won the 2018 North American Cup Consolation at Mohawk Raceway with Courtly Choice, one of the top three-year-olds of 2018. Also, to his credit, James won the $300,000 Roses are Red with world champion Lady Shadow and the $150,000 Battle of the Belles at Grand River, but his 2017 World Driving Championship must rate at the top of his career highlights.

The World Driving Championship, the climax of a series of races across Canada against many of the best drivers in the world, was a spectacular affair for race fans. With the final leg in Charlottetown, the race drew big crowds not only to the track but also to wherever the drivers went. The eighth and final leg of the 2017 World Driving Championship was set for Friday of Gold Cup and Saucer week, and a packed crowd of approximately 18,000 jammed into Red Shores for the final races. When the dust had settled, James emerged as the 2017 World Driving Champion with more points than the other eight drivers from harness racing countries around the world. Marcus Miller of the United States finished second while Mike Forss of Finland finished third overall.

James travelled to Sweden in May, 2019 to defend his world title, but it was not to be; Rick Ebbinge from The Netherlands took the title in the five-track Sweden competition with the final round at the Solvallo track in Stockholm.

Curtis MacDonald, a non-driver-trainer, is also carving out quite a name for himself in the video production and harness racing business. Curtis, who helped train horses part-time

James MacDonald captured the 2017 World Driving Title, the first ever for PEI, in front of an enormous crowd at Red Shores Charlottetown.

James gets a big hug from his mom Gail

Amy and Anthony MacDonald pose with the prestigous Cam Fella Award at the 2018 O'Brien Awards , the first ever for a PEI trainer-driver.

for Anthony in the early days at Campbellville, has been the Racing Products and Solution Specialist for Online Media and Entertainment since 2006. In that role, Curtis looked after harness and thoroughbred tracks all over North America. He now has his own company—Cujo Entertainment—and is extremely busy but always there for Anthony and the live events at The Stable.Ca and Tomiko Training Centre. Curtis has worked with Dome Productions in televising the World Junior Hockey tournament in Halifax, the Gold Cup and Saucer in Charlottetown, and more recently with his own company Cujo Entertainment, the Cavendish Beach Festival in PEI. He is also responsible for the COSA (Central Ontario Standardbred Association) harness racing productions, all the content, and manages all their social media channels in addition to similar work with Harness Racing Update. At last month's O'Brien Gala, Curtis produced the Red Carpet portion of the O'Brien Awards hosted by Kelly Spencer and co-produced the O'Brien Awards with the Woodbine Group.

Curtis MacDonald watches drone at The Stable.Ca training centre.

The MacDonald Boy's today :
Scott MacDonald, Tex, Fred "Fiddler", Sandy, Sock, Rabs, Sput MacDonald.

The girls take time out from lunch for this Charlottetown 2019 photo:
Left to Right, Jamie Ellen, Ramona, Bernadine, Peggy and Monica.

Mark, Lloyd, Fred, Anthony, Gail, James, Curtis and Bobby.

Tex, dad, mom and Fred at UPEI graduation.

Dave Mackenzie and Lee Drake of Red Shores Charlottetown present banner to members of the MacDonald family on the occasion of driver Mark MacDonald joining the $100,000,000 career earnings club in August, 2020- the first Islander to reach that lofty mark. In the picture are Rabs MacDonald, his wife Anita, Gail MacDonald and Fred MacDonald, Mark's parents.

Over the past two decades, the MacDonald boys have been piling up accolades in the North American harness racing game. The June 2018 edition of *Hoof Beats*, the major USA harness racing magazine, featured an extensive story called "Booming Brood" part of which follows below:

Here is Howie Trainor's "Introduction":

After starting in Charlottetown, PEI, and spreading across the continent, the MacDonalds are arguably the first family of North America harness racing. Fred and Gail, known as dad and mom, still live in Charlottetown. Their family now extends to Ontario and New York and includes a world driving champion, multiple stakes and two-time O'Brien Award winner for Canadian driver of the Year, a trainer-driver-businessman whose innovative idea for attracting new owners is revolutionizing the harness racing industry, a Toronto based simulcasting expert, an Ontario businessman who also works on equine video projects, and a Maritime farrier and horse owner.

Fred is a newspaper columnist and publisher of the *Atlantic Post Calls* racing periodical. He's owned and bred dozens of horses, including some outstanding trotters. Gail has been the track photographer at Red Shores Charlottetown in Charlottetown for thirty years and has long been involved in industry initiatives. Fred's column in the Charlottetown *Guardian,* which has a harness racing component, is a must read. His philosophy is to be fair, call it as you see it and don't be shy about voicing your opinion. It's been a successful formula for forty years. (*Hoof Beats*, June 2018)

The year 2020 was another successful year for the MacDonald brothers in the race game. Mark, who had been sidelined for seven months after a spill that required shoulder surgery, captured the $250,000 Graduate at the Meadowlands on July 11 in spectacular fashion. In this one, Mark had positioned Hurricane Emperor second over and when the field turned for home, he asked his pacer to respond. The Hurricane blew away the field including Dancin' Lou, Bettors Wish, Century Farroh,

James MacDonald wins the $540,000 Canadian Pacing Derby with Dorsoduro Hanover in 1:48 and change at Mohawk, July, 2020.

Mark MacDonald drives Hurricane Emperor to sizzling 1:47 victory in the 2020 Graduate at the Meadowlands and biggest slice of the $250,000 purse

and six others, the mile in 1:47, fastest of the year to that time.

"This is beyond words," said trainer John McDermitt, "through this pandemic has been such a torture, all I did was go deeper in the hole. Thank God for my partners who have supported me because it has not been easy. I really thought he was going to be awesome tonight and Mark gave him the most beautiful drive in the world."

Less than two months later, on September 5 at Mohawk Raceway, James was in the spotlight and he also was barely recovered from a spill. The $540,000 Canadian Pacing Derby attracted the best aged pacers in America, minus Hurricane Emperor who was sick. James got the driving assignment on Dorsoduro Hanover from the Ron Burke stable. This race turned into a speed duel as the leaders Bettors Wish, Century Farroh, and Sintra battled on the front most of the way. James waited until the head of the long Mohawk stretch, then unleased Dorsoduro Hanover who won going away in 1:48:4.

Later in the fall, on November 24 at Dover Downs, Anthony drove Jazzy Judy to victory in the $100,000 Delaware Standardbred Breeders two-year-old trot. Anthony, who prefers trotters over pacers, stayed in the pocket most of the way tipping to the outside at the top of the lane, and trotting home in a lifetime best of 1:59:4 for owners The Stable Jazzy Judy Group in Guelph, Ontario.

CHAPTER 20

The Five-Minute Flurry

ALMOST EVERY RESIDENT OF PEI WATCHED CBC IN THE evening, especially between 2009-2017 when ratings peaked usually on Monday evenings during the airing of "The Five-Minute Flurry." The program was the idea of producer Tracy Lightfoot. Bruce Rainnie was the host and I was his weekly guest for nine years, and we did not hesitate to voice our opinions on a wide range of sports' topics. It would be difficult to find a better anchor than Bruce whose knowledge of sports almost exceeded mine. Bruce likely believes otherwise.

Meeting Bruce and starting with CBC Compass was a stroke of good luck on my part. I hadn't been in radio or on television nor did I expect to be. Nevertheless, one afternoon in 2009, I received a call from CBC to join Bruce and an old friend from my race track days, Kevin "Boomer" Gallant for a trial run of a short five-or-ten-minute TV show on sports. Most harness racing fans in Atlantic Canada knew Boomer as the voice of the Charlottetown Driving Park, and he attracted a huge following. I was one of them.

Since sports were right up my alley, I decided to take Boomer's advice, and give it a shot. Bruce was the ideal coach and teacher. He also had plenty of patience: half-way through one of the takes, Bruce interjected, "Let's start over again. You know you can't say that in television. You'll get fired. And don't make any references to God. Got it?"

A few weeks later, and again half-way through Bruce called a halt: "We have to start again. You can't say that about what the coach reminds you of." And off we'd go again.

I astonished myself and most likely Bruce too by completing the first six months with higher and higher ratings after every show, so much so that Bruce felt he should reduce the cast to just the two of us and embark on a new show called "The Five-Minute Flurry." Boomer too was all for the move, which made it a smooth transition since we were long-time friends.

There were occasions on the show, many of them, when Bruce burst into laughter and had to stop, pointing out my mistake and shout, "Ok, take #2," "take #3," or perhaps "take #4." On rare occasions, Bruce would cause the re-take, but mostly, it was a lot of fun.

Bruce Rainnie and Fred MacDonald just prior to CBC Charlottetown segment of Five Minute Flurry

One of the most memorable shows that we did where the legal people got involved was the piece where Bruce asked me about my opinion on the possibility that another Quebec Major Junior hockey franchise might be headed to Summerside. My comment was something like, "Bruce, any relocation to Summerside would have to be approved by the Board of the Governors of the Quebec League, and since most are friends of Serge Savard Sr. who owns the Charlottetown franchise, it is highly unlikely they will move another team to PEI." However, I didn't stop there, I continued, "Who do you think the Board will listen to, Serge Savard Sr. who, when he speaks on hockey matters in Montreal, it's like the finger of God pointing at you. Will the people listen to Serge or those bozos up in Summerside who gave away $1 million dollars for a Michael Jackson concert that never took place?"

The following week, CBC allotted Basil Stewart, Summerside's Mayor, time for his comments on the "Five-Minute Flurry," saying approximately, "Fiddler called it as he saw it and signed his name to it, unlike those others who hide behind false names in social media." Basil and I often chuckle over the skirmish.

Few people are immune to Bruce's charm; however, fortunately for the show, I was not one of the many, at least on air. Bruce knew what buttons to push to fire me up. Plus, the audience loved it when Bruce and I would take opposite sides of a trade or sports story and, sometimes, I would come out on top. Among the many things I learned about Bruce was how diligently he prepared. Whether on our sports show or with any guests he had on Compass, Bruce usually knew as much or more about the subject than the guest. It was a tremendous advantage.

However, Bruce and I do have our differences. By nature, he is not combative and I am. He is diplomatic where I might be more apt to draw the sword and take a slice out of the hide of those who consistently made bad plays or decisions. The combination was ideally suited for television and for the show. People still ask when Bruce and I are going to do the show again.

Bruce often assisted in occasional charitable fundraisers, and he frequently took me along as his sidekick. One such occasion, we helped with a fundraiser on behalf of the Tignish Pee Wees, which was headed to the Quebec International tournament. Unbeknownst to Bruce, I had a couple of conditions on my attendance for the evening: I would speak first, Bruce last, and upon completion of my talk, organizers were to make sure my wine glass was never empty of red wine. Team organizers Sheila Gaudet and Nicole Morrison came through.

Since Bruce is not a drinker, I did not want to take any alcohol with me on the journey back to Charlottetown as that would not be allowable with Bruce. I had a plan. I requested that one of the organizers fill my container not with pop but with red wine and a straw so that Bruce would not know the difference. By the time we got to Summerside, Bruce said, "For God's sake, man, you've asked me that same question three times since we left Tignish." It was my last long trip on the Island with Bruce.

In June 2017, Bruce's departure for Halifax as President and CEO with the Nova Scotia Sports Hall of Fame and Boomer's retirement at the same time left a huge hole in the CBC Compass program. The ratings for The Five Minute Flurry, which was seen across Canada and the USA by many Islanders living away, and, as I found out later, by Islanders working in China, had created an enormous following.

There have been many long-serving CBC television news personalities and anchors stationed in Charlottetown over the years such as Roger Younker, the late Matt Campbell, and Wayne Collins. Bruce Rainnie, who took over as anchor of the supper-hour *Compass* show in November 2003 and stayed until May 2017, carved out a great reputation on the Island and was a much-loved personality. He and his wife Kendra, a talented violinist, started their family here: boys Mark 10 and Allister 7. Bruce likes to remind me that his boys can't be called CFAs. I have always told Bruce, Islanders by choice or Islanders by birth: we are all the same.

Bruce and I still communicate via e-mail and sometimes by phone. We also make a point of having lunch whenever we are in the same city at the same time. As for Boomer, I touch base with him occasionally in Charlottetown, like Bruce, a lifetime friend.

CHAPTER 21

That's a Wrap

WHILE MY BOYS CONTINUE THEIR HARNESS-RACING careers "up-country," my brothers and I are winding down our careers here in Charlottetown. Tex, who retired from teaching and guidance work at Colonel Gray, left the second career as assistant to former Premier Robert Ghiz, and now sticks to active involvement in amateur sports. He had been the first head football coach at Holland College when the college revived football and coached the baseball Charlottetown Islanders retiring from the senior baseball Islanders in 2017 to take up his new love—golf—with modest success. Tex has two boys and a girl: Matt played university football at Mount Allison, Ian is a local businessperson, and Stephanie, who starred in soccer at St. Francis Xavier University, is an Emergency Room nurse who just completed the requirements as a Nurse Practitioner.

Rabbit and his wife Anita believe Curtis is their boy and that's good too. He's retired from his position as store manager at the PEI Liquor Commission, and is currently working with his long-time friend Al Stewart in the office at A & S Scrap Metals.

Sput and his wife Elva (Ellis) have two talented daughters— Laura and Emily. Laura works in the health department with Dr. Heather Morrison, and Emily works for Air Canada.

Sandy is President of Holland College, and is married to Barb MacLeod, daughter of the late Charlottetown lawyer

Dave MacLeod. They have two children: Jessica who has a Masters degree from St. Mary's University and works in Halifax, and Max who is currently attending Concordia University in Montreal.

Sock is still Moosehead Breweries manager for PEI. His daughter is Megan, who holds a Masters degree in social work from the University of Toronto. She married Ryan O'Keefe and they have a boy named Drew Fiddler and a new girl named Mora Mary.

Scott and his wife Heidi (MacIntyre) live in Summerside where he is a school principal. They have two sons, Colin who graduated from Dalhousie and lives in Halifax, and Brodie who lives in Charlottetown and attends UPEI.

Many people on PEI are surprised when they hear that the MacDonald family also includes six distinguished sisters.

Bernadine (MacDonald) Boadway resides in Kingston, Ontario, and is a retired R.N. She graduated in 1965 from the Charlottetown School of Nursing. She is a very good singer, and was a talented piano player in her youth. She is married to Robin Boadway, a Rhodes Scholar and Economics professor at Queens University in Ontario.

He and Bernie have two boys: John is a corporate patent lawyer in Toronto, and Andrew works in Kingston. In the summer months, Bernie and Robin come home to Stanhope and are members of the Stanhope Golf Course when not playing tennis.

Ramona (MacDonald) Taylor is now a semi-retired lab technician at UPEI. In her teens, she excelled in track and field and, had rugby been a sport in her school days, she would have been a star. She and her husband Errol have three daughters, Alana, a prominent Charlottetown lawyer, and Carolyn and Ellen who are talented school teachers.

Peggy (MacDonald) Devine went to the Canada Games as a gymnast in her teens and high school years. Now retired from human resources with the federal government, Peggy lives with her husband Kevin Devine, director of player personnel with the Buffalo Sabres.

Jamie Ellen MacDonald resides in Charlottetown with her husband Bob Golliher and their daughter Monica. Jamie Ellen was a top athlete in her youth and her daughter Monica excels in volleyball and basketball at the senior high level. Jamie Ellen is the CAO of the Queen Elizabeth Hospital, and is a certified healthcare executive with over eighteen years' senior leadership experience in both domestic and international healthcare.

My youngest sister Monica MacDonald attended university locally and in Europe. She is an archeologist and the Manager of Research at the Canadian Museum of Immigration at Pier 21 in Halifax. She holds a PhD in communications and culture, and is a gifted writer who wrote *Recasting History: How CBC Television Has Shaped Canada's Past* in 2019, published by McGill Queens Press.

Recently, I toured our old paper routes with my long-time friend Wally McInnis and we reminisced about the costs of things today as compared to 50-60 years ago. It is hard to imagine that we sold newspapers for three cents years ago and today the Saturday edition of *The Guardian* sells for $2.25. Wally chuckled, "If things keep going up, we may have to start up the shoe-shine business again." It could happen.

I am still writing—on Saturdays only—for *The Guardian*. Gail and I are co-editors of the *Atlantic Post Calls*, which covers harness racing in Atlantic Canada, Quebec, and Ontario, and features stories from up-country, and this book of memories.

Time only knows whether any of the Fiddler grandsons/ granddaughters will continue the MacDonald legacy in sports and/or harness racing. It is likely that at least one of the following will choose the harness racing game for a career; Anthony and Amy have Ava, Oliver and Adeline; Mark and Alea have Kiara "Kiki" plus Marshall and Connor; Curtis and Jaimi have Lennon; while James has Griffin. It is not likely that Lloyd's Elizabeth who is an RN, and Robert who works in business with his dad will be in the race game, nor will Alexander, Bobby and Patrice's boy. Nevertheless, one never knows as neither of the Fiddlers contemplated a career in harness racing for them or their kids.

I suppose in another two decades, Tex and I will be gone as well many of our brothers and sisters, but until that day arrives, all I can tell you is enjoy and love life with friends and family.

Special thanks to my wife Gail for her patience and support, to Lee Ellen Pottie, publisher Terrilee Bulger, and old friend Lorne Yeo and for graphic artist Cassandra Aragonez.

This book is in loving memory of mom and dad, Pat and Fiddler, who would have enjoyed this journey and for my brothers and sisters who have helped make this story a wonderful experience.

Endnotes

1   SDU received a provincial degree-granting charter in 1917, but did not actually award its first bachelor's degrees until the spring 1941 convocation. SDU was affiliated with Université Laval, awarding joint degrees from the 1890s onward. Following the decision to start granting its own degrees, SDU severed the relationship with Laval by 1956. https://saint-dunstansuniversity.ca/about/history/

2   Windsor, Lee A. (2003) "Too Close for the Guns!" 9 Canadian Infantry Brigade in the Battle for Rhine Bridgehead," Canadian Military History: Vol. 12: Iss. 2, Article 2. Available at: http://scholars.wlu.ca/cmh/vol12/iss2/2

3   Dad's military information was taken from his attestation, medical, and military personal records obtained from Library and Archives Canada.

4   *The Guardian*'s Lorne Yeo covered the many meetings of the Steering Committee, which led to the formation of UPEI that year. It was "us Catholics against them Protestants!"

5   Nifty Smyth was a great baseball guy, very knowledgeable about the game, and well known in Toronto baseball circles; he was instrumental in the development of 2012 Cincinnati Reds superstar Joey Votto, who played in his early teens for Nifty in Toronto. Nifty now scouts for Major League baseball out of British Columbia, I believe. He came to visit me in the early 1970s with his wife at the time but I had forgotten about his coming to PEI, and left for Edmonton and a fastball tournament the day before he arrived. There were no cell phones then, and I was extremely upset at not being on the Island for Nifty's visit.

6   Richard Bradley was one of the great caretakers in North America and worked for Stanley Dancer for many years. He and his partner Peggy supervised the Little Brown Jug paddock for numerous years. Richard passed away in Ohio, October 2018.

 FRED "FIDDLER" MACDONALD is the son of James L. Fiddler MacDonald who was a university athlete and a baseball pitcher. He married Patricia Bradley before joining the Canadian Army and serving at the Battle of Blenheim, 1945. After the war, Fiddler Senior worked at various jobs until finding full-time employment with Canada Post until his retirement. He and Pat had 14 children; a crib death resulted in raising 13 children, seven boys and six girls. This is their story as well as the story of a post-war East Coast city and the burgeoning sports teams of the area.